SpringerBriefs in Applied Sciences and Technology

PoliMI SpringerBriefs

More information about this series at http://www.springer.com/series/11159
http://www.polimi.it

Mariagrazia Fugini · Enrico Bracci
Mariafrancesca Sicilia
Editors

Co-production in the Public Sector

Experiences and Challenges

POLITECNICO
DI MILANO

Editors
Mariagrazia Fugini
Department of Electronics, Information and
   Bioengineering
Polytechnic of Milan
Milano
Italy

Mariafrancesca Sicilia
Department of Management, Economics and
   Quantitative Methods
University of Bergamo
Bergamo
Italy

Enrico Bracci
Department of Economics
University of Ferrara
Ferrara
Italy

ISSN 2191-530X   ISSN 2191-5318 (electronic)
SpringerBriefs in Applied Sciences and Technology
ISSN 2282-2577   ISSN 2282-2585 (electronic)
PoliMI SpringerBriefs
ISBN 978-3-319-30556-1   ISBN 978-3-319-30558-5 (eBook)
DOI 10.1007/978-3-319-30558-5

Library of Congress Control Number: 2016939106

Printed on acid-free paper

This Springer imprint is published by Springer Nature
The registered company is Springer International Publishing AG Switzerland

Preface

This book is the result of a scholarly discussion started during the Workshop "Co-production and public services" organized by the ICONA research centre at the University of Milan (Italy) in mid-2014. It aims at presenting a short but up-to-date analysis of what co-production is and the different forms in which it manifests in the planning, design and delivery of public services.

Co-production has always existed in public services, but its theoretical relevance was lately recognized, thanks also to the change of paradigm in public management. Indeed, the traditional Public Administration (PA) and the New Public Management (NPM) paradigms do not foresee any particular role of citizens and communities in the public service policy and management. On the contrary, the Public Governance (PG) paradigm started to contend PA and NPM, in considering citizens, non-profit organizations and communities having a relevant, if not an equal, role in designing and delivering public services.

Despite the development in the literature and among practitioners, co-production is far from being a clear and undebated phenomenon, but it is rather a dynamic and magmatic matter. However, the austerity policies and post-NPM reforms are changing heavily the role of public agencies. Nowadays, public services are not only delivered by professional and managerial staff in public sector organizations but are also co-produced, to some extent, by citizens (individuals and groups), non-profit organizations and communities.

Co-production is considered a form of public service management in order to increase the level of effectiveness and efficacy, with stable or even reduced public resources. In order to achieve these promises, several aspects need to be taken into account, some of which can be problematic.

The contributions of this book present and discuss some of these elements in an essential and direct manner, giving an overview of the literature in some paradigmatic areas, and leveraging best practices and/or case studies. Some of the explored fields are social care, health care, employment services and smart cities. Moreover, we debate how technology can support a clearer definition of co-production and encourage its adoption.

The editors are thankful to the authors, and to the anonymous reviewers, as well as to the many contributors who, directly and indirectly, debated and worked with us on applications and studies in some of the illustrated fields of interest, such as health care and social services, services to employment and smart environments. Besides ICONA and its participants, we mention Fondazione Politecnico for cooperation on Attiv@bili, Prof. Piercarlo Maggiolini (Politecnico di Milano) and Prof. Ramon S. Vallés (UPC) for the case study on services to employment, our various colleagues working in adjacent fields who contributed in various ways—and often unaware—to our analysis of the subject.

This volume is dedicated to our families and ... to the "world of services".

Mariagrazia Fugini
Enrico Bracci
Mariafrancesca Sicilia

Contents

Chapter 1
Co-production of Public Services: Meaning and Motivations

Enrico Bracci, Mariagrazia Fugini and Mariafrancesca Sicilia

1.1 Introduction

Today, many governments are looking for new ways to create, design and deliver public services. In this context, co-production is playing a central role becoming a key element of current public service reforms in many countdries around the world and at all levels of government. Consequently, over the last years, it has gained attention from public management scholars who have been debating on several aspects, ranging from what co-production is, to its value and benefits.

This book is a collection of chapters that focus on *co-production in public services*. The general purpose is to enhance the knowledge on this topic providing examples of co-production in different organizational settings and fields such as health, social care as well as smart cities and employment services sectors, and discussing their critical issues and implications for practice.

By tackling the concepts of co-production, co-management and co-governance as a conceptual framework that enables us to understand recent developments, we discuss how co-production is related to public service design, concept, development, use, maintenance and evolution. Therefore, we examine co-production in all the life-cycle of a public service, from its conception to its deployment and disposal, which is one of the novel aspects of this book.

In this first chapter, we want to show the historical evolution of the concept of co-production, illustrating how the role of citizens has changed in public service

E. Bracci (✉)
University of Ferrara, Ferrara, Italy
e-mail: enrico.bracci@unife.it

M. Fugini
Polytechnic of Milan, Milano, Italy

M. Sicilia
University of Bergamo, Bergamo, Italy

© The Author(s) 2016
M. Fugini et al. (eds.), *Co-production in the Public Sector*,
PoliMI SpringerBriefs, DOI 10.1007/978-3-319-30558-5_1

delivery over the decades in the three main models of public administration. Then, given that the existing knowledge about co-production is fragmented and heterogeneous, in this book we aim to clarify the concept and to delimit it by explaining what co-production is and what co-production is not.

This chapter is organized as follows. We review the main models of public administration and co-production in Sect. 1.2 Then we debate on what co-production is and is not in Sect. 1.3. Finally, we give an overview of the book contents in Sect. 1.4.

1.2 The Main Models of Public Administration and Co-production

After its first emergence in the 1970s, thanks to the research activity of Elinor Ostrom and her colleagues from Indiana University, *co-production* has waxed and waned over the decades, being added to the institutional arrangement available to public sector organizations only recently, in the post-*New Public Management* (NPM*)* era (Alford 2009).

Until the end of the 1970s, the dominant management paradigm in public administration, referred to as 'old public administration', was based on control, well-defined rules, hierarchy, and bureaucracy. In this paradigm, on the one hand governments directly provide services to the public; on the other hand, as suggested by (Hartley 2005), the population is assumed to be 'fairly homogenous' and its role is conceived as the role of a 'client'. Citizens play a passive role, whereas public organizations are the *active participant* in the exchange relationship.

Later, the 'old public administration' model was replaced by the New Public Management (NPM) model (Dunleavy 2005). Along with NPM, came the idea that government should be run in a business-like manner (Ferlie et al. 1996). In terms of public services management, NPM prompted a new model inspired by market orientation and with a focus on performance, privatization and contracting—in and —out of services. Accordingly, as specified in (Denhardt and Denhardt 2000), 'the common theme in the myriad of applications of these ideas has been the use of market mechanisms and terminology, in which the relationship between public sector organizations and their consumers is understood as based on self-interest involving transactions similar to those occurring in the market place'. The NPM model is coherent with a vision of the *population* as *consumer of public services* rather than as a client (Hood 1995). Consumers are expected to perform more aware and selective choices among the various providers of public services, and even to quit providers, in case they are not satisfied.

More recently, the 'new governance model' (Bingham et al. 2013) has spread. It recognizes that public service delivery relies on complex and articulated relationships between public organizations and other actors. This model emphasizes a more pluralistic and plural model of provision of public services based on networks,

Table 1.1 Public service provision in the three main models of public administration

Public service provision	Old public administration model	New public management model	New governance model
Organizational values	Hierarchy, control and bureaucracy	Market orientation, focus on performance, contracting in-out	Networks, inter-organizational relationships and multi-actor policymaking processes
Role of the population	Client	Consumer	Co-producer

inter-organizational relationships, and multi-actor policymaking (Agranoff and McGuire 2003; Huxham and Vangen 2005; Stoker 2006). In this model, citizens are not merely recipients of services, but rather are invited to act as co-producers not only at the operational stage of the service production process, where their contribution is an essential component of service delivery (Osborne and Strokosch 2013), but also at the strategic and design stage.

Thus, it is in the post-managerial era that co-production is conceived as an option that 'can add to the repertoire of institutional arrangements available to public sector organizations in seeking to achieve their purposes' (Alford 2009). This option relies on the idea that people outside the public administration represent 'huge untapped resources' and that their mobilization can trigger radical innovation in public services (Boyle and Harris 2009). In this vein, professionals are required to work in a more flexible way turning their attention from inwards issues to outwards issues, working collaboratively with their citizens.

What explained until here is sketched in Table 1.1.

Several reasons account for the current importance given to co-production. One reason is the increase of demand of complex services for wicked problems (Head and Alford 2013). Another reason is the need to provide public services that are better targeted and more responsive towards users (Duffy 2007). Third, there is the need of squeezing budgets in the widespread status of austerity of public finance and the related need of cutting costs (Grimshaw 2013; Bracci et al. 2015). Finally, we mention the challenges resulting from growing democratic and citizenship deficits.

1.3 What Co-production Is and What It Is Not

Co-production is far from being a new concept. It has been in used in different guises since the 1970s (see for instance Gartner and Riessmann 1974; Gersuny and Rosengren 1973). The initial idea was that in a service society, the customer becomes an important factor in the production of services. In the context of *public services*, co-production has been defined and discussed under different perspectives and facets. Starting from the seminal work conducted by Elinor and Vincent

Ostrom and colleagues, it is argued that the *collaboration* between the *supply side* and the *demand side* of services is a key aspect in achieving the desired results (outputs and outcomes) in most public services (Ostrom and Ostrom 1977).

According to Osborne and Strokosch (2013), co-production is not an additive quality of public services, which may be optionally present, but rather a core future attribute of public services. *De-facto*, in several public services, such as health and social care, education or the like, it is undisputed that the clients become part of the production process and the outcome of the intervention is partly dependent on them (Brudney and England 1983). If such wide definition and view were adopted, any occasion of citizens/clients involvement in public services would be considered co-production, then limiting the conceptual, practical and political significance. Any effort to define a conceptual artifact needs to be convincing not just in terms of logical development but also of in terms of usefulness to academics and practitioners alike (Brudney and England 1983).

Consequently, it is important to define what co-production is as well as what it is not. Defining the contours of the concept and its core elements is the base for any fruitful research.

In this book, the aim is to provide a customized and up-to-date definition of co-production, highlighting the commonalities and differences among the main available definitions. The aim is also to propose the key elements that characterize the concept of co-production, as well as what co-production *is not*.

Starting from the initial work conducted by Ostrom and colleagues, co-production was originally defined as 'the mix of activities that both public services agents and citizens contribute to the provision of public services. The former are involved as professionals, or 'regular producers', while 'citizen co-production' is based on voluntary efforts by individuals and groups to enhance the quality and/or quantity of the services they use' (Parks et al. 1981).

Consistently, Brudney and England (1983) consider co-production whenever the citizen is involved, or participates, in the delivery of public services on a voluntary basis, in order to improve the outcomes, also through *active behavior*. The authors proposed three possible types of co-production: *individual*, *group* and *collective*. Analogously, Pestoff (2012) classifies the acts of co-production in relation to the fact that users act as an individual or a group. In details, the author proposes:

(1) Individual acts of co-production.
(2) Collective acts of co-production.
(3) A mix of individual and collective acts of co-production.

Bovaird proposes the following definition: 'the provision of services though regular, long-term relationships between professionalized service providers (in any sector) and service users and or other members of the community, where all parties make substantial resource contributions' (Bovaird 2007). In this definition, the regularity and long-term relationship is stressed as central in a co-production situation.

Alford defines co-production as 'any active behavior by anyone outside the government which: is conjoint with agency production, or is independent of it but prompted by some action of the agency; is at least partly voluntary; and, either intentionally or unintentionally creates private and/or public value, in the form of either outputs and outcomes' (Alford 2009). According to Alford, in order to identify co-production, two elements should be present:

(1) Co-production must involve creation of public value, together with possible private value.
(2) Co-production should contribute to both outputs and outcomes, where outcomes can come beforehand, since there could be co-production even with no production of a specific output.

More recently, Osborne and Strokosch (2013) propose an extension to the co-production concept by combining different streams of literature (i.e., service management, public management and public administration).

They thus conceptualized *three modes* of co-production:

- *Consumer co-production* (located in the service management area).
- *Participative co-production* (located in the public administration and public management areas).
- *Enhanced co-production* (which combines elements of the two previous modes to produce a third hybrid mode).

Operational co-production is simply the consequence of the inseparability of the moments of production and consumption in many public services. *Strategic (or participative) co-production* involves the willingness among users/citizens and public service professional to design new ways of delivering services to improve the quality and the level of the achieved outcomes. Finally, the authors propose the idea of *enhanced co-production,* where operational and strategic modes are combined in order to innovate and transform public services (p. 37).

Co-production is often used in a general way by referring to different patterns and modes of citizens' participation (individually, or in organized forms) in public service provisioning, policy making and policy implementation. Indeed, according to Pestoff (2012), it is possible to talk about co-production in a strict sense, of

Table 1.2 Different meanings and concepts of co-production

Typology	Content
Co-production	Arrangement where citizens produce their own services, in total or in part. It can also end out in alternative service delivery by citizens, with or without state intervention, but with public funding
Co-management	Arrangement between the third sector and public agencies and for-profit actors to deliver services in collaboration with other actors
Co-governance	Arrangement where the third sector, along with public agencies and for-profit actors is involved in decision making and planning of public services

Modified from (Pestoff 2012)

Table 1.3 Clients/citizens and public servants' roles and co-production

		Responsibility for design of public services		
		Public servant	Public servant and clients/citizens	Clients/citizens
Responsibility for delivery of public services	Public servant	1. Traditional service provision	2. Mixed (co-production on design side)	3. Public servant as a sole deliverers
	Public servant and clients citizens	4. Mixed (co-production on the delivery side)	5. Full co-production	6. Mixed (co-production on the delivery side)
	Clients/citizens	7. Clients/citizens delivery of a professionally designed service	8. Mixed (co-production on design side)	9. Self-organized client/citizens provision

Modified from Bovaird (2007: p. 848), Boyle and Harris (2009: p. 16) and Ryan (2012: p. 316)

co-management and co-governance (see Table 1.2), in relation to which phase of the public service policy process the 'co-' is involved in.

In a similar vein, Bovaird (2007) propose a definition of co-production that can be located unambiguously in the area of planning and delivery of public services, throughout the policy process. Consequently, co-design, co-management, co-delivery and co-assessment can all together represent a *specific aspect of the overall shift* towards an increased diffusion of co-production (Bovaird 2007).

Co-design and other forms of requiring user involvement may be ending in creating the space for co-production. However, without a *continuity* in the *involvement* and in the *delivery relationship*, it may end up in something, which is close to, but different from, co-production. In the view of Boyle and Harris (2009), co-production occurs when public servants or professionals and clients/citizens are involved in a voluntary relationship combining both the design and the delivery of a service (see Table 1.3). Any other combinations may represent mixed versions of co-production, more oriented either to the *design* of service or to the *delivery* of services.

Brandsen and Honingh (2015) proposed the following definition of co-production, as: "*a relationship between a paid employee of an organization and (groups of) individual citizens that requires a direct and active contribution from these citizens to the work of the organization*" (p. 5). Such definition points out three main characteristics of what co-production is: the presence of a continuous relationship between the employees of an organization and the individual citizens (or group); the direct and active inputs and efforts of the citizens; and the voluntary engagement of the citizen, and the payment of the employee. The authors reckon the existence of varieties of co-production according to the level of involvement of the citizens and the proximity of the tasks that the citizens perform to the core service of the organization.

This conceptual schema and definitions are helpful since they make it clear what co-production is, as well as what it is not. In particular, co-production *is not* (Boyle and Harris 2009):

- *Consultation of users*: soon after listening to users, the professionals take in charge the delivery of the service.
- *Volunteering*: co-production is more than just volunteering, since when citizens co-produce, they do not just contribute with resources, but they also consume the provided services (Alford 1998; Bovaird 2007) donating time to perform some activity on behalf of the public organization, but it requires reciprocity and exchange in the design and delivery of the service.
- *Giving users direct money as support*, e.g., to personalize their care: this means discharging the responsibility for the design and delivery of the service to the clients, without a sustaining networks of public and private actors.

Let us consider now *what co-production is*. In most of the existing definitions in the literature, the following seem to be the main elements, in particular (Brudney and England 1983; Bovaird 2007; Alford 2009; Pestoff 2012; Ryan 2012; Brandsen and Honingh 2015) *co-production* is:

1. A voluntary (unpaid) and not coercive or normatively set.
2. An active rather than passive involvement of users.
3. Focused on public value creation in terms of outcomes as well as of outputs.

Moreover it:

4. Should encompass the *whole policy process* (from design to delivery).
5. Requires *interdependency* among the involved actors, both in terms of supplied inputs and provided information, and of achievement of outcomes.
6. Has to be *transformative*, for the professionals and for all the involved actors. It hence becomes a different way of thinking and performing public services.
7. Should be *innovative* and able to cope with the *changing technology and needs*.
8. Fosters the *sustainability and resilience of public services*. Co-production may mobilize new resources, most of private type, and find ways for doing more with less.

The above elements are vital in the current economic period of austerity in many European and non-European countries. The traditional welfare state is put into question, and so is the way public services are designed and delivered (Grimshaw and Rubery 2012). The new social economy (Murray 2009; Murray et al. 2010) requires a change from the old model based on production and consumption to a model based on distributed networks to sustain and manage relationships with blurred boundary between producers and consumers (Grimshaw 2013).

If this is the present and the near future, it is necessary to bear clear in mind what co-production is, what its constituting elements are and what the conditions for its existence are.

1.4   Book Contents

The various contributions are autonomous but connected by a common background of the authors gained through common studies, workshops and conferences, work and/or projects and consultancy in the public sector, as well as from personal acquaintance and cooperation.

The idea of the volume is to bring together various themes related to co-production so as to enhance our knowledge on the basis of a multi-perspective approach.

In Chap. 2, Sancino and Jacklin-Jarvis offer a critical discussion of the concepts and practices of co-production and inter-organizational collaboration in the provision of public services. These two concepts may often be confused and often overlap. The authors propose four main types of relations between co-production and inter-organizational collaboration in the provision of public services. They conclude with some implications of these different relationships, proposing interesting further avenues of research on co-production and inter-organizational collaboration and the relationship between the two in practice.

In Chap. 3, Barbera et al. focus on a specific accounting tool, namely participatory budgeting, discussing the conditions under which it can be considered a form of co-production. Participatory budgeting, they argue, should allow citizens to influence public decision on the allocation of public resources to different public programs, services and investments. Barbera et al. present four conditions for successfully implementing participatory budgeting as a form of co-production, namely: interaction, inclusiveness, responsiveness, and representation.

On a vein similar to what presented in Chaps. 2 and 3, Bracci and Chow, in Chap. 4, consider the theme of personalisation of social care in England. Indeed, despite its growing ubiquity, personalisation is not well defined as yet, and what, if any, links to personal budgets are is still being debated. The authors discuss the trends in personalization in England and to what extent which personalisation and co-production are related and/or overlap. Co-production appears as a style of service "life" which often flows underneath a system design or operation, but does not emerge explicitly until some studies bring it to the surface. Studies and experience, particularly those of the authors, contribute to determine the common denominator lying under various systems design activities.

In Chap. 5, authored by Bassani et al., a case of co-production in the health and social care domain is presented and discussed. In their analysis, the authors provide a framework through which scholars and practitioners could pinpoint actions, processes, structures and intangible aspects (i.e. factors) related to co-production at "operational" level and "strategic" level. Besides, the framework considers peculiar factors that enhance co-production at both levels.

The following Chap. 6, authored by Gilardi et al., covers the application of co-production in the healthcare sector. In particular, it is argued that the pressure towards co-produced health services is increasing as an answer to quality improvement and system sustainability. The chapter tracks the evolution of the concept of co-production in healthcare, by reconstructing the shift in thinking from the original patient engagement framework. Co-production is considered a complex system of multiple relations between a variety of both single (i.e., patients) and collective actors (i.e., healthcare providers). The above issues are discussed through the empirics derived from selected case studies, some recommendations for the healthcare managers, useful for promoting and sustaining the development of such co-production practices, are thus developed.

Overall, the chapters devoted to health and social care collectively demonstrate that moving towards added-value services coproduced with users and citizens might ameliorate the performance of the services.

The Book ends with a specific focus on the role of ICT in fostering the development of co-production. In Chap. 7, Castelnovo discusses how co-production can be applied to smart cities. Making cities smarter appears to be the technological fashion both for politician, public and private managers, and academics. This chapter provides an informed overview of the characteristics of a Smart City and the implications for the human and technology. It then focuses on the role of citizens as sensors/information providers and on the way for citizens to participate in smart city initiatives. The author argues that citizens as sensors/information providers can act as co-producers only if they are given back the control over their user-generated information, and that the development of a user-centric personal data ecosystem is an enabling condition for citizens' participation in smart city initiatives as sensors/information providers.

The contribution by Fugini and Teimourikia, in Chap. 8, focuses on services in e-government. It is based on use cases in two areas, namely services to employment and services for integrated social care. In services to employment, co-production is shown to be a hidden but determinant factor in the design of automated tools for job matching: making stakeholders aware of the users' involvement in the design and development of services contributes to the success or failure of a whole system. The second use case, namely the Attiv@bili project, shows how ICT and co-production have been merged from the initial phases of the development. Overall, the authors contend that the main issue is about how it is possible to operationalize innovation given the increasing number and range of stakeholders engaged in co-producing innovation, addressing common challenges. The main issues are in maintaining effort for high ambition targets and the potential for stakeholders to become enrolled in different initiatives.

The whole set of contributions in the book demonstrates that co-production is not a zero-sum process though: it requires education, skills, proper tools, awareness and responsibility from both governments and citizens. Thus, the expected benefits are not guaranteed, but when properly managed co-production might generate not only better services for the service users, but also values for the community as a whole improving for example democratization, transparency and responsiveness. Although this book adds to the existing knowledge about co-production, further research is needed to delve deeper the indented and unintended effects of co-production and to develop a more systematic perspective on the challenges to the traditional institutional structures and processes, systems of accountability and governance.

References

R. Agranoff, M. McGuire, Inside the matrix: Integrating the paradigms of intergovernmental and network management. Int. J. Public. Adm. **26**, 1401–1422 (2003). doi:10.1081/PAD-120024403

J. Alford, A public management road less travelled: Clients as co-producers of public services. Aust. J. Public. Adm. **57**, 128–137 (1998)

J. Alford, Engaging Public Sector Clients, in *From Service-delivery to Co-production* (Palgrave Macmillan, Basingstone, UK, 2009)

L.B. Bingham, R.O. Leary, L. Blomgren Bingham et al., The new governance: Practices and processes for stakeholder and citizen participation in the work of government. Public Adm. Rev. **65**, 547–558 (2013). doi:10.1111/j.1540-6210.2005.00482.x. The new governance: Practices and processes for stakeholder and citizen participation in the work of government

T. Bovaird, Beyond engagement and participation: User and community co-production of public services. Public Adm. Rev. **67**, 846–860 (2007)

D. Boyle, M. Harris, *The Challenge of Co-production* (London, 2009)

E. Bracci, C. Humphrey, J. Moll, I. Steccolini, Public sector accounting, accountability and austerity: more than balancing the books? Account. Audit. Account. J. **28**(6), 878–908 (2015). doi:10.1108/AAAJ-06-2015-2090

T. Brandsen, M. Honingh, Distinguishing different types of coproduction: A conceptual analysis based on the classical definitions. Public Adm. Rev. (2015). doi:10.1111/puar.12465

J. Brudney, R.E. England, Toward a definition co-production concept. Public Adm. Rev. **43**, 59–65 (1983)

R.B. Denhardt, J.V. Denhardt, The new public service: Serving rather than steering. Public Adm. Rev. **60**, 549–559 (2000). doi:10.1111/0033-3352.00117

S. Duffy, The economics of self-directed support. J. Integr. Care **15**, 26–37 (2007). doi:10.1108/14769018200700012

P. Dunleavy, New public management is dead-long live digital-era governance. J. Public. Adm. Res. Theory **16**, 467–494 (2005). doi:10.1093/jopart/mui057

E. Ferlie, L. Ashburner, L. Fitzgerald, A. Pettigrew, *The New Public Management in Action* (Oxford University Press, Oxford, UK, 1996)

A. Gartner, F. Riessmann, *The Service Society and the Consumer Vanguard* (Harper and Row, New York, 1974)

C. Gersuny, W. Rosengren, *The Service Society* (Schenkman Publishing, Cambridge, MA, 1973)

D. Grimshaw, Austerity, privatization and levelling down: public sector reforms in the United Kingdom, in *Public Sector Shock*, ed. by D. Vaughan-Whitehead (Edward Elgar and ILO, London, 2013)

D. Grimshaw, J. Rubery, The end of the UK's liberal collectivist social model? The implications of the coalition government's policy during the austerity crisis. Cambridge J. Econ. **36**, 105–126 (2012). doi:10.1093/cje/ber033

J. Hartley, Innovation in governance and public services: Past and present. Public Money Manag. **25**, 37–41 (2005). doi:10.1111/j.1467-9302.2005.00447.x

B.W. Head, J. Alford, Wicked problems: Implications for public policy and management. Adm. Soc. (2013). 0095399713481601. doi: 10.1177/0095399713481601

C. Hood, The "new" public management in the 1980s: Variations on a theme. Account. Organ. Soc. **20**, 93–109 (1995)

S. Huxham, C. Vangen, *Managing to Collaborate* (Routledge, London, 2005)

B.R. Murray, Danger and Opportunity, in *Crisis and The New Social Economy* (London, 2009)

R. Murray, J. Caulier-Grice, G. Mulgan, *The Open Book of Social Innovation* (NESTA, London, 2010)

S.P. Osborne, K. Strokosch, It takes two to tango? Understanding the co-production of public services by integrating the services management and public administration perspectives. Br. J. Manag. **24**, S31–S47 (2013). doi:10.1111/1467-8551.12010

V. Ostrom, E. Ostrom, Public Goods and Public Choices, in *Alternatives for Delivering Public Services: Toward Improved Performance*, ed. by E.S. Savas (Westview Press, Boulder, Colorado, 1977)

R.B. Parks, P.C. Baker, L. Kiser et al., Consumers as co-producers of public services: Some economic and institutional considerations. Policy Stud. J. **9**, 1001–1011 (1981). doi:10.1111/j.1541-0072.1981.tb01208.x

V. Pestoff, Co-production and Third Sector Social Services in Europe, in *New Public Governance, the Third Sector and Co-production*, ed. by V. Pestoff, T. Brandsen, B. Verschuere (Routledge, New York, 2012)

B. Ryan, Co-production: Option or obligation? Aust. J. Public Adm. **71**, 314–324 (2012). doi:10.1111/j.1467-8500.2012.00780.x

G. Stoker, Why Politics Matters, in *Making Democracy Work* (Palgrave Macmillan, 2006)

Chapter 2
Co-production and Inter-organisational Collaboration in the Provision of Public Services: A Critical Discussion

Alessandro Sancino and Carol Jacklin-Jarvis

2.1 Introduction

The concept and the practice of co-production is gaining considerable attention among scholars, professionals, policy makers and by society in general (e.g. Boyle et al. 2010; Harris and Boyle 2009; Verschuere et al. 2012). However, there is also theoretical and analytical confusion about what co-production is, as pointed out in Chap. 1. In particular, one element of confusion is the relationship between co-production and inter-organisational collaboration. For example, the Organisation for Economic Co-operation and Development (OECD) defined co-production as 'a way of planning, designing, delivering and evaluating public services which draws on direct input from citizens, service users and civil society organizations' (OECD 2011), and some scholars endeavour to link co-production and inter-organisational collaboration within a single analytical framework (Poocharoen and Ting 2015).

However, one distinctive of co-production is that it specifically involves citizens in public service delivery—whether at individual, group, or collective level (Brudney and England 1983). Brandsen and Pestoff (2006) offered a first clear taxonomy of co-production and inter-organisational collaboration through the concepts of co-management and co-governance: co-management describes an arrangement where third sector organisations deliver services in collaboration with the State, while co-governance indicates an arrangement where third sector organisations participate both in the design and delivery of public services.

With this book chapter, we aim to offer a further critical analysis of the concepts of *co-production* and *inter-organisational collaboration* and discuss some implications of this distinction. More specifically, we describe and analyse the two concepts, we offer emergent conceptualizations of the relationships between them, and we illustrate conceptualizations with case examples. As two scholars coming

A. Sancino · C. Jacklin-Jarvis (✉)
Open University Business School, Milton Keynes, UK
e-mail: c.e.j.jarvis@open.ac.uk

© The Author(s) 2016
M. Fugini et al. (eds.), *Co-production in the Public Sector*,
PoliMI SpringerBriefs, DOI 10.1007/978-3-319-30558-5_2

separately from the co-production and inter-organisational collaboration literatures, we assert the importance of both distinguishing between co-production and inter-organisational collaboration and more clearly articulating the relationships between the two.

The reasons why we think that this topic is particularly relevant are at least three. Firstly, as Pestoff (2012) affirms, there are different levels of analysis in the co-production debate and, in our view, it is beneficial to provide a contribution that clearly locates inter-organisational collaboration and co-production at different levels of analysis. Secondly, we are observing an increasing trend from professionals in embracing those terms in an overlapping ways: however, this blurring has the potential to obscure both different aspects of the relationships between actors (including the power dynamics which underlie the conceptual models) and implications for practice. Thirdly, turning attention towards the actors of co-production can deepen the discussion about "the publics" in public service delivery (Thomas 2013).

The structure of the chapter is the following. Sections 2.2 and 2.3 provide a theoretical backdrop to the discussion of co-production and inter-organisational collaboration. Section 2.4 summarizes the main differences between the two concepts, going on to explore the relationships between the two in practice. Section 2.5 presents some final reflections and provides future research perspectives.

2.2   Co-production of Public Services: A Theoretical Backdrop

The phenomenon of co-production is definitely not new; however, the term co-production was coined by the Economics Nobel Prize winner Elinor Ostrom in the late 1970s to explain and give theoretical foundation to practices concerning 'the involvement of ordinary citizens in the production of public services' (Pestoff 2012, p. 1105). Chapter 1 highlighted that there are many definitions of co-production: all the definitions are pretty similar, but some elements deserve further debate.

For example, Ostrom (1996) talked about co-production of a good or a service; Bovaird (2007) emphasized the issue of regular, long-term relationships; Pestoff (2009) distinguished among dimensions of citizen participation in the provision of public services; Brandsen and Honingh (2015) added the adjective direct in defining citizen participation. Put more simply, co-production is still a maturing concept (Pestoff et al. 2009).

However, even within a rich and variegated debate, it is possible to formulate some statements that can help to synthesize the main advancements in the scientific debate around the nature of co-production of public services:

- for many public services, co-production is an inherent feature that is not a matter of choice (Brandsen and Honingh 2015; Parks et al. 1981, 1999; Whitaker 1980);
- co-production of public services may happen at every level of government (OECD 2011) and in contexts increasingly characterized by multi-level governance settings (Sicilia et al. 2015), and it is particularly relevant for public services delivery at the local level (Brudney 1983), this being the level closest to citizens;
- there are some policy fields that are particularly co-production intensive, such as health, education, environment, safety, leisure, welfare (OECD 2011);
- co-production may happen at different stages of the public service cycle (Bovaird 2007; OECD 2011; Sicilia et al. 2015) and is about doing something (Alford 2013), in other words it captures the role that citizens can and do play in the actual provision of services (Brudney and England 1983);
- '*rather than trying to determine one encompassing definition of the concept, several different types of coproduction can be distinguished*' (Brandsen and Honingh 2015, p. 1);
- co-production of public services is different from co-production of goods (Ostrom 1996) or co-production of public outcomes (e.g. Alford 2013; Bovaird and Loeffler 2012);
- co-production of public goods and/or outcomes happens at the meta-level and requires a more complex approach encompassing other kinds of activities beyond co-production, such as, for example, peer-production and inter-organisational collaboration (Sancino 2016).

2.3 Inter-organisational Collaboration for Public Services: A Theoretical Backdrop

The management literature uses the term collaboration to describe a range of activities and entities, which extend across organisational boundaries. Organisational actors 'work together', 'partner', 'network' and 'cooperate', through inter-organisational entities, including 'coalitions', 'federations', 'joint ventures' and 'partnerships' (Cropper et al. 2008). These activities and entities facilitate inter-organisational relationships, which enable organisations to share resources, tangible and intangible, in order to achieve their objectives. Those objectives may include innovation, market development, supply chain integration, and, in the public arena, delivering 'joined-up' services, and addressing complex social problems, which require the resources of organisations from across sector boundaries. In this chapter, we focus on collaboration in the provision of public services.

In summary, inter-organisational collaboration has four key elements (Cropper et al. 2008):

- the organisations;
- the relationship between them;
- the enactment of that relationship through processes—at the micro level (interactions between individuals), and at the macro level (the development of collaboration over time as it is impacted by key environmental factors);
- the context within which the inter-organisational relationship is enacted.

In the public services context, collaborative public managers act together with actors within and beyond the public sector to develop innovative approaches to social problems, and deliver services, which tackle those problems (O'Leary and Bingham 2009; O'Leary and Vij 2012). To enable this collaborative relationship and to deliver services which appear 'joined-up' or 'seamless' to service users, public agencies establish partnerships, joint working groups, informal and formalised inter-agency and cross-sector arrangements, through which organisational actors interact, build trust, and develop relationship (Cropper et al. 2008; Vangen and Huxham 2003).

Following the definitions offered by Huxham and Vangen (2005) and Agranoff and McGuire (2003), we define *collaboration* as a situation in which individual actors work together across organisational boundaries in a sustained way to achieve something which they could not achieve alone. The literature refers to this as 'collaborative advantage' (Huxham and Vangen 2005). In the context of public service delivery, 'collaborative advantage' is frequently understood in terms of the delivery of integrated services, which make effective use of limited public resources, avoid artificial silos, and offer users an experience of seamless service provision (Glasby et al. 2011).

Clearly, inter-organisational collaboration in the public service domain takes place for a number of inter-related purposes, including policy development and governance at the strategic level. While, our focus here is on the provision of public services, in practice, these purposes maybe closely interwoven, fluid, and ambiguous.

The actors in such collaborative efforts frequently include representatives of (more or less formal) user and citizen groups, as well as formalised third sector organisations, alongside public sector actors. They may also increasingly include private sector actors. Research shows that the collaboration membership and allegiance of individual actors may be ambiguous (Huxham and Vangen 2000): individuals may be citizens, community members, and service users, as well as organisational representatives. For example, a residents' support group may create a third sector organisation and employ a coordinator precisely because he/she lives in the local community. In the context of an inter-agency working group tasked with delivering services within that community, this coordinator is *both* an organisational representative *and* an individual citizen who may be directly impacted by those services.

While the potential for bringing together the different knowledge, expertise and resources of public agencies and third sector organisations to produce services is clear, research also captures the challenges and limitations of collaborating across organisational and sector boundaries. These include:

- the complexity of managing the 'tangled web' of individual, organisational, and inter-organisational goals (Vangen and Huxham 2012);
- the tendency of inter-organisational partnerships to make painfully slow progress due to organisations' competing interests, and consequently to fall into inertia (Huxham and Vangen 2004);
- the tensions associated with collaborating in a competitive environment (Milbourne 2009);
- the challenges of maintaining organisational independence, and the potential for co-optation into the public sector agenda (Lewis 2005).

Consequently, inter-agency collaboration is by no means a panacea for delivering services to meet social needs (Dickinson and Glasby 2010; Glasby et al. 2011). However, in an age of limited public resources, there is also an acknowledgment that collaboration across organisational and sector boundaries is an inevitable feature of the public service landscape. For the purposes of our discussion, we can identify the following attributes of collaboration as significant for public service delivery:

- collaboration, as defined here, is inherently inter-organisational.[1] As a consequence, collaboration actors are both enabled and constrained by the organisational context;
- collaboration is enacted by individuals and through their interactions. Those individuals act on behalf of their organisation, but may themselves be community members, citizens, service users and/or service professionals;
- collaboration is enabled and constrained by collaborative entities. For example, the structures and terms of reference of working groups and partnership bodies frame the processes through which organisations and their representatives interact;
- collaboration is relational. It depends on the building of trust, but also on compromises and trade-offs which enable the relationship to continue in spite of competing interests.

We also note that collaboration for the purposes of integrated service delivery is closely related to (and in practice may be inseparable from) collaboration which enables multiple voices to be heard in the processes of understanding social needs and developing strategies to address those needs. Lewis's (2005) analysis of partnership working under the UK's New Labour government of 1997–2010 notes the tension this produces for third sector organisations who are service deliverers, but also endeavour to facilitate citizen participation.

---

[1]We are not here concerned with the other streams of the literature on collaborative management, which may also focus—among the others—on the role of managers in working in groups and teams with a collaborative style.

2.4 Relationships Between Co-production and Inter-organisational Collaboration in the Provision of Public Services

We can now highlight some main distinctions between the concepts of co-production and inter-organisational collaboration:

i. co-production and collaboration can be understood as situated at different levels within the context of public services provision. Drawing on Alford and O'Flynn (2012), we can characterise inter-organisational collaboration and co-production as drawing on different modes of coordination between actors in the processes of public services provision. More specifically, in co-production public managers and/or professionals coordinate with service users and citizens directly through the building of trust but also through a process of exchange at the individual, group and/or collective level, with an immediate impact on the service experience. In inter-organisational collaboration, coordination also proceeds through a process of trust building—but this must extend beyond individuals to the collaborating organisations, which may also relate to one another through formal contracting arrangements. The impact on the experience of the service user is therefore an indirect one.

ii. inter-organisational collaboration is a broad concept, which, in the sphere of public services, is applied to a range of entities (e.g. partnerships, working groups, forums) with a range of purposes. While some of these can be said to adopt a shared approach to service production, others have a different remit—from information sharing to strategy development and collaborative governance.

iii. in co-production, individual actors are citizens at the individual, group and/or collective level that both as users or volunteers give a direct and active contribution to the provision of a public service. They do not act as representatives of an organisation, but rather bring their expertise as service users to the processes of service design and delivery. This input is direct and unmediated. In contrast, collaboration is an inherently inter-organisational phenomenon, within which individuals participate on behalf of their organisation, whilst endeavouring to achieve a common purpose across organisational boundaries. In collaboration, organisational context bounds the individual actor's engagement.

Therefore, in general terms we could say that the actors and purposes of collaboration and co-production are different. More specifically, these differences relate to the relationship between actors and service provision and the relationship between modes of coordination, actors, and organisations. However, in practice, we suggest that the distinction between co-production and inter-organisational collaboration may not be so clear. Indeed, co-production and inter-organisational collaboration may be in place at the same time: as Pestoff et al. (2006, p. 592) wrote, *systems of provision increasingly combine different mechanisms of co-ordination and different types of actors.* Nevertheless, the literature on co-production and inter-organisational collaboration have so far downplayed this issue, employing a silo perspective and focusing mainly separately on one or the other phenomenon.

We recognise four possible relationships between co-production and inter-organisational collaboration in the provision of public services:

- co-production as an antecedent of inter-organisational collaboration;
- inter-organisational collaboration as an enabler of co-production;
- co-production and inter-organisational collaboration as distinct but complementary;
- co-production and inter-organisational collaboration as alternative strategies.

In the following section, we explore these relationships, illustrating them through an extended example, which draws on our own experiences in public management and as researchers. We draw our example[2] from the social services field, as this is an area of service delivery, which exemplifies the significance of the direct relationship between professional and service user, but in which user-focused third sector organisations also play a critical role.

2.4.1 Co-production as Antecedent of Inter-organisational Collaboration

Below we introduce our case example and illustrate the first relationship between co-production and inter-organisational collaboration, in which co-production is an antecedent of inter-organisational collaboration.

Box 2.1: From co-production to inter-organizational collaboration: an example

Alice and Bill's son Thomas is severely autistic, and has limited communication skills. The family receives services from the department of services to children of the local authority. This department adopts a co-production approach to service design and delivery.

Alice and Bill work in close cooperation with the local authority staff to provide services, which support the whole family, engaging with Thomas's social worker in the design and delivery of services to meet their specific needs. These services include respite provision, and an agreed approach to behaviour management, which is implemented together by parents and the

---

[2]This is a fictionalized example which draws on our combined experiences and observations. One of us worked in local authority children's services departments and in third sector organisations for 20 years before researching cross-sector collaboration: the other worked as a local councillor in two local authorities for nine years and had experience as a member of the board of directors in several third sector organisations before working as an academic researcher in the public management field.

local authority service provider. The social worker convenes regular meetings between professionals and parents, in which Alice and Bill are regarded as expert members of the team. They contribute to the selection of carers, and to the planning of Thomas's activities and therapies, which are delivered consistently across respite and home care. The local authority also provides Alice and Bill with opportunities to meet with other parents of autistic children by providing the resources for a parent self-help group. Alice and Bill find this group a useful source of support and information.

As Thomas reaches the teenage years, Alice and Bill begin to feel that the services provided no longer meet Thomas's needs, and specifically that Thomas needs to engage in activities with young people of his own age. They also find Thomas's behaviour increasingly difficult to manage, and are concerned that inconsistencies are arising between their own approach to behaviour management and that adopted by respite carers. They raise these issues with the social worker, who explains that the local authority is currently unable to make changes to Thomas's care package due to resource limitations.

Again, Bill and Alice find support and ideas in talking over their concerns with other parents within the self-help group, and a small group of parents decides to formalise this support group, adopting a basic constitution. Later, this group becomes a registered charity, named PLUS, providing the structure to employ a part-time staff member, Jill, who supports parents to advocate with the local authority, inputting into the continued design and delivery of services.

In this scenario, inter-organisational collaboration is a product of the practice of co-production. A parent-led organisation develops as a direct result of the challenges of engaging in co-production, and the parents' need for support. Such user-led organisations develop from the recognition that the relationship between users and professionals contains an asymmetry of power. They empower service users and their families to engage in the co-production process, and in this context, the inter-organisational relationship between PLUS and the local authority is entirely focused on the purpose of enabling parents to co-produce services. This leads to our second understanding of the relationship between coproduction and collaboration.

2.4.2   Inter-organisational Collaboration as an Enabler of Co-production

Box 2.2: Inter-organizational collaboration can empower users for co-production of public service

PLUS has grown from a small self-help group to an advocacy group for parents of autistic children. Bill and Alice find that engaging with PLUS enables them to contribute more effectively to the design and delivery of services for Thomas and for their family. PLUS offers opportunities for confidence building and for skills development for parents, including training in assertiveness, public speaking, and group work, as well as informal support and information exchange. Over time, with the support of PLUS, Bill and Alice become more confident and assertive, and better informed, in their personal engagement with the local authority. They are more confident in their own expertise, and more willing to challenge local authority staff when they disagree. In their conversations with local authority staff, they regularly assert the value of PLUS in enabling them and other parents to engage in this way.

PLUS is invited by the local authority to join an inter-agency working group, which is planning future service provision. A parent representative and a worker of PLUS, Jill, both join this group. Therefore, they are able to provide parents with information and insight into key challenges, decisions and opportunities which they can make use of during the ongoing co-production of services for their families. Through the inter-agency group, parents learn about the number of teenagers with autism, their level of need, and their location around the local authority area. This provides them with the information they need to develop a weekly youth group, funded by resources identified through the inter-agency group.

In this scenario, collaboration between a user-led a third sector organisation and the local authority enables co-production. PLUS enables and empowers parents in their co-production role, and amplifies their voice by ensuring that their concerns are expressed through the formal collaboration of the working group. Through its collaboration with the local authority, PLUS increases the exchange of information and knowledge between the local authority and parents, builds the capacity and skills of its members, and increases the resources and mechanisms for participation in service production.

2.4.3 Co-production and Inter-organisational Collaboration as Distinct but Complementary

Box 2.3: Co-production and inter-organisational collaboration in the same system with different aims

PLUS is now an established third sector organisation with a key role on the inter-agency working group which oversees the delivery of services for autistic children and their families across the locality. PLUS's part-time worker, Jill, is frequently consulted by local authority managers. When invited, she also joins discussions between parents and local authority staff.

During this period of development, PLUS becomes a member of a national federation of parent-led organisations which liaises with the local authority on the strategic development of children's services, and campaigns at the national level for the parent voice in services for autistic children. The parent-led board of PLUS continues to run the recently developed youth group for autistic young people, and is considering whether to bid to provide other services through the commissioning processes of the local authority.

The work of PLUS has a continuous impact on the design and delivery of services used by Thomas and his family through its input to the strategic development of services, its campaigning work, and direct service provision. At the same time, Bill and Alice continue to work directly with Thomas's social workers to ensure that services that meet the family's specific needs, are delivered.

Here we see the potential for co-production and inter-organisational collaboration to co-exist at different levels in the system of provision of public services: more specifically, in this situation inter-organisational collaboration influences the provision of public services through advocacy. This points to the fact that the two phenomena may act as distinct but complementary processes in the provision of public services; they operate at different levels of advocacy and service (co)production, but both impact on the provision of public services.

However, it is worth saying that there are also potential tensions in the relationship between co-production and inter-organisational collaboration. While third sector user organisations may be perceived as essential by service users and their families, the perception of local authority staff may be more complex as the organisation becomes a stronger advocate. In addition, there is a risk that over time the concerns of organisational life may cause the organisation to become increasingly disassociated from the parents themselves.

In our example, the relationship, which began as an unmediated one between parents and professionals, is now affected by organisational and inter-organisational context, and is subject to all of the risks of inter-organisational collaboration, including the potential for collaborative inertia (Huxham and Vangen 2004). In this perspective, it is important to remember that third sector organisations frequently see their role, not simply as alternative service providers, but also as a means to provide a voice for citizens and service users. At their best, they empower citizens to play a role in service production: at their worst, they have the potential to disempower citizens by mediating that voice through the lens of organisational interests.

2.4.4   Co-production and Inter-organisational Collaboration as Alternative Strategies

Finally, public sector professionals may view co-production and inter-organisational collaboration as alternative strategies for providing public services. For example, a social worker may decide to design and deliver social services with individual users, or with third sector organisations representing or encompassing users. Drawing on the definitions explored here, each of these strategies has somewhat different implications in terms of the relationship between public services and their users. Public service delivery through co-production becomes a strictly 'public' way of designing and implementing public services, with an immediate and direct relationship between professional(s) and service user(s) and the service delivered. In contrast, the provision of public services through inter-organisational collaboration may be understood as a hybrid way of designing and implementing public services. This involves actors from third and/or private sectors bringing their resources to the shaping and co-delivery of services in ways that reflect the interests of service users and communities, but also take account of organisational interests and concerns.

This distinction has implications for current debates on the main paradigms of public administration. More specifically, it is pertinent to debates relating to new public governance, to the outsourcing of public services, and to the relationship between public services and the public. For example, from a public sector perspective, an instrumental view of collaboration with third sector organisations tends to focus on the potential for outsourcing. Such outsourcing may offer a narrative of service provision which is closer to service users and communities, but has also the potential to mask continuing public sector control of service production through the commissioning process. Consequently, as a strategy for public service managers, collaboration with third sector organisations *may* be a means to empower users in the service production process, but also has the potential to *disempower* users as they are distanced from the service production process.

In other words, while inter-organisational collaboration is often associated with new public governance, the change in the balance of power between users, public sector, and third sector organisations, which such governance arrangements imply, are by no means automatic. When power is too unequally distributed among collaborating entities, relationships based on trust are replaced by regulation and hierarchy which reinforces asymmetric relationships between the state, third sector organisations, and the public (Milbourne and Cushman 2013). This concern is implicit in some of the criticism which arose around the debate on the political manifesto of Big Society in the UK, which could also be seen for some elements as the resurgence of principles and ideas not so far from the privatizing and outsourcing wave of New Public Management (Pestoff 2015). We do not have the space here to fully enter in this debate: the main point is that, as framed here, co-production and inter-organisational collaboration are distinct phenomena, which point towards issues of ideology and power, which are pertinent to the decision to engage in these alternative strategies for the provision of public services.

2.5   Conclusions

This book chapter summarizes the main distinctions between co-production and inter-organisational collaboration in the provision of public services, but also offers a more complex view of the relationships that the two phenomena may have in provision of public services. As a consequence, if we embrace a more systemic and dynamic view of public services provision, we can see that—even with different actors, purposes and modes of coordination—the relationship between co-production and inter-organisational collaboration may become more nuanced and complex, potentially underlying important issues in the provision of public services, such as the role of power in the relationships between public agencies and external providers of public servicers (Alford and O'Flynn 2012) and the potential of developing social capital for the latter in engaging with public agencies.

In this perspective, as Pestoff et al. (2006) noticed, an interesting question is how different combinations of co-production and inter-organisational collaboration are and should be embedded, given the variations in national structures of service provision. Future research should thus attend to the patterns of relationships between co-production and inter-organisational collaboration in the provision of public services. Research should consider dealing more explicitly with the relationships between users and informal community groups, formalised third sector organisations, and citizens (Rochester 2013) to clarify in what circumstances and in what ways different types of third sector organisations might enable or constrain co-production.

Moreover, we suggest that the concept of *power* has all too often been hidden in the discourses of both co-production and collaboration. It is important that the issue of power is surfaced in a future research agenda focused on relationships between public sector professionals, third sector organisations and citizens in the design and delivery of public services, as well as the impact on social and institutional capital of co-production and inter-organisational collaboration.

In practical terms, we suggest that there is a need for public managers to attend to the power dynamics of both co-production and inter-organisational collaboration, and to the ways in which each of these enables the voice of users and communities in service production (or not). From this perspective, co-production and collaboration may be seen as interwoven strategies for practice, which together have the potential to enable empowered relationships between professionals and citizens at multiple levels within the service production process, but which may also mask more traditional hierarchical relationships.

References

R. Agranoff, M. McGuire, *Collaborative Public Management: New Strategies for Local Governments* (Georgetown University Press, Washington DC, 2003)
J. Alford, Engaging Citizens in Co-producing Service Outcomes, in *Putting Citizens First*, ed. by E.A. Lindquist, S. Vincent, H. Wanna (The Australian National University, Canberra, 2013)

J. Alford, J. O'Flynn, *Rethinking Public Service Delivery* (Managing with external providers, Palgrave, London, 2012)

T. Bovaird, Beyond engagement and participation: User and community coproduction of public services. Public Admin. Rev. **67**(5), 846–860 (2007). doi:10.1111/j.1540-6210.2007.00773.x

T. Bovaird, E. Loeffler, From engagement to co-production: The contribution of users and communities to outcomes and public value. Voluntas, **23**(4), 1119–1138 (2012). doi:10.1007/s11266-012-9309-6

D. Boyle, A. Coote, C. Sherwood, J. Slay, Right Here, Right Now: Taking Coproduction into the Mainstream. (Nesta (National Endowment for Science, Technology and the Art), London, 2010)

T. Brandsen, M. Honingh, Distinguishing different types of coproduction: A conceptual analysis based on the classical definitions. Public Admin. Rev. (2015) doi:10.1111/puar.12465 (In press)

T. Brandsen, V. Pestoff, Co-production, the third sector and the delivery of public services. Pub. Man. Rev. **8**(4), 493–501 (2006). doi:10.1080/14719030601022874

J. Brudney, R.E. England, Toward a definition coproduction concept. Public Admin. Rev. **43**(1), 59–65 (1983)

S. Cropper, M. Ebers, C. Huxham, P.S. Ring, Introducing Inter-organizational Relations, in *The Oxford Handbook Of Inter-organizational Relations*, ed. by S. Cropper, M. Ebers, C. Huxham, P.S. Ring (Oxford University Press, Oxford, 2008)

H. Dickinson, J. Glasby, Why partnership working doesn't work: Pitfalls, problems and possibilities in English health and social care. Public Admin. Rev. **12**(6), 811–828 (2010). doi:10.1080/14719037.2010.488861

J. Glasby, H. Dickinson, R. Miller, Partnership working in England—where we are now and where we've come from. Int. J. Integr. Care, **11**(Special 10th Anniversary Edition), 1–8 (2011)

M. Harris, D. Boyle, *The challenge of co-production* (New Economics Foundation and NESTA, London, 2009)

C. Huxham, S. Vangen, Ambiguity, complexity and dynamics in the membership of collaboration. Hum. Relat. **53**(6), 771–806 (2000). doi:10.1177/0018726700536002

C. Huxham, S. Vangen, Realizing the advantage or succumbing to inertia? Organ. Dyn. **33**(2), 190–201 (2004)

C. Huxham, S. Vangen, *Managing to Collaborate: The Theory and Practice of Collaborative Advantage* (Routledge, London, 2005)

J. Lewis, New labour's approach to the voluntary sector: Independence and the meaning of partnership. J. Soc. Policy **4**(2), 121–125 (2005). doi:10.1017/S147474640400226X

L. Milbourne, Remodelling the third sector: Advancing collaboration or competition in community-based initiatives? J. Soc. Policy **38**(2), 277–297 (2009). doi:10.1017/S0047279408002845

L. Milbourne, M. Cushman, From the Third Sector to the Big Society: How changing UK government policies have eroded third sector trust. Voluntas, **24**(2), 485–508 (2013). doi:10.1007/s11266-012-9302-0

OECD, *Together for Better Public Services: Partnering with Citizens and Civil Society* (OECD Publishing: OECD Public Governance Reviews, Paris, 2011)

R. O'Leary, L.B. Bingham (eds.), *The Collaborative Public Manager: New Ideas For The Twenty-First Century* (Georgetown University Press, Washington, D.C, 2009)

R. O'Leary, N. Vij, Collaborative public management: Where have we been and where are we going? Am. Rev. Public Adm. **42**(5), 507–522 (2012). doi:10.1177/0275074012445780

E. Ostrom, Crossing the great divide: Coproduction, synergy, and development. World Devel. 24 (6), 1073–1087 (1996). doi:10.1016/0305-750X(96)00023-X

R.B. Parks, P. Baker, L. Kiser, R.J. Oakerson, E. Ostrom, V. Ostrom, S.L. Percy, M. Vandivort, G. P. Whitaker, R. Wilson, Consumers as co-producers of public services: Some economic and institutional considerations. Policy Stud. J., 9 Summer, 1001–1011. Reprinted 1999 in M.D. McGinnis (ed.), *Polycentric governance and development: Readings from the workshop in political theory and policy analysis* (University of Michigan Press, Ann Arbor, MI, 1981)

V. Pestoff, Towards a paradigm of democratic participation: Citizen participation and co-production of personal social services in Sweden. Ann. Public Coop. Econ. **80**(2), 197–224 (2009). doi:10.1111/j.1467-8292.2009.00384.x

V. Pestoff, Co-production and third sector social services in Europe: Some concepts and evidence. Voluntas **23**(4), 1102–1118 (2012). doi:10.1007/s11266-012-9308-7

V. Pestoff, Co-production at the Cross-Roads. Keynote speech. IIAS Study Group on Co-production of Public Services, Radboud University, Nijmegen (NL), 8–9 May 2015

V. Pestoff, S.P. Osborne, T. Brandsen, Patterns of co-production in public services. Pub. Man. Rev. **8**(4), 591–595 (2006). doi:10.1080/14719030601022999

O. Poocharoen, B. Ting, Collaboration, coproduction, networks—convergence of theories. Pub. Man. Rev. **17**(4), 587–614 (2015). doi:10.1080/14719037.2013.866479

C. Rochester, *Rediscovering Voluntary Action: The Beat of a Different Drum* (Palgrave, Basingstoke, 2013)

A. Sancino, The meta coproduction of community outcomes: Towards a citizens' capabilities approach. Voluntas, **27**(1), 409–424 (2016). doi:10.1007/s11266-015-9596-9

M. Sicilia, E. Guarini, A. Sancino, M. Andreani, R. Ruffini, Public services management and co-production in multi-level governance settings. Int. Rev. Adm. Sci. Published online on 5 June 2015. doi:10.1177/0020852314566008

J.C. Thomas, Citizen, customer, partner: Rethinking the place of the public in public management. Public Admin. Rev. **73**(6), 786–796 (2013). doi:10.1111/puar.12109

S. Vangen, C. Huxham, Nurturing collaborative relations: Building trust in inter-organizational collaboration. J. Appl. Behav. Sci. **39**(1), 5–31 (2003). doi:10.1177/0021886303039001001

S. Vangen, C. Huxham, The tangled web: Unraveling the principle of common goals in collaborations. J. Public Adm. Res. Theory **22**(4), 731–760 (2012). doi:10.1093/jopart/mur065

B. Verschuere, T. Brandsen, V. Pestoff, Co-production: The state of the art in research and the future agenda. Voluntas, **23**(4), 1083–1101 (2012). doi:10.1007/s11266-012-9307-8

G.P. Whitaker, Coproduction: Citizen participation in service delivery. Public Admin. Rev. **40**(3), 240–246 (1980). doi:10.2307/975377

Chapter 3
The Participatory Budgeting as a Form of Co-production

Carmela Barbera, Mariafrancesca Sicilia and Ileana Steccolini

3.1 Introduction

Co-production in the public realm is not necessarily limited to the delivery of public services, and extends to the full chain of service planning, design, managing, delivering, monitoring, and evaluation activities (Bovaird 2007; Sicilia et al. 2015). In particular, *co-planning* refers to collaborations and networking between the public sector and its stakeholders (i.e., citizens, associations, interest groups, etc.), aimed at identifying what services need to be provided to answer stakeholder needs, whereas *co-design* refers to interactions in decision-making processes on operational production of services and their evaluation (Pollitt et al. 2006).

This chapter is aimed at looking at participatory budgeting as a form of co-production, and, more specifically, as a form of co-planning and co-design. Specifically, it proposes a framework, which identifies the conditions for successfully implementing participatory budgeting as a form of co-production.

Participatory budgeting is "a decision-making process through which citizens deliberate and negotiate over the distribution of public resources" (Wampler 2007, p. 21). Thus, through participatory budgeting, citizens have the opportunity to influence public decisions on the allocation of public resources (see also Krenjova and Raudla 2013; Lerner 2011; Rossmann and Shanahan 2012; Steccolini 2004;

C. Barbera (✉)
The Catholic University of the Sacred Heart, Milano, Italy
e-mail: carmela.barbera@unicatt.it

C. Barbera
SDA Bocconi School of Management, Milano, Italy

M. Sicilia
University of Bergamo, Milano, Italy

I. Steccolini
Bocconi University, Milano, Italy

© The Author(s) 2016
M. Fugini et al. (eds.), *Co-production in the Public Sector*,
PoliMI SpringerBriefs, DOI 10.1007/978-3-319-30558-5_3

Zhang and Liao 2011). This can allow prioritizing social issues and holding government accountable for how resources are spent.

Participatory budgeting is seen as an important tool for increasing democracy and reaching greater political involvement at the local level (Ebdon and Franklin 2006; Pinnington et al. 2009; Lerner 2011; Rossmann and Shanahan 2012). It may also promote greater levels of accountability and transparency (Pinnington et al. 2009; Lerner 2011; Krenjova and Raudla 2013), reducing opportunities for corruption (Pinnington et al. 2009). It is furthermore associated with greater efficiency and with making people more connected to their city (Lerner 2011).

The use of participatory budgeting began in 1989 in the Municipality of Porto Alegre, Brazil, from the political campaign based on democratic participation of the Workers' Party. The aim of that experience was to improve the conditions of less affluent citizens, increasing the levels of public spending to be allocated for answering their needs. Since then, at least 1500 experiences of participatory budgeting have developed around the world (Baiocchi and Ganuza 2014).

There is no standard model of participatory budgeting (Sintomer et al. 2008); extant experiences are different based on the political, social and economic contexts in which they developed. In general terms, participatory budgeting experiences share the preliminary identification of needs and priorities, a deliberation, a decision making process and the implementation of projects selected by citizens (Pinnington et al. 2009; Lerner 2011). However, differences may exist on the way citizens are involved during the preparation of the budget, and on how, after the approval of the budget, the projects are implemented (Sintomer et al. 2008; Krenjova and Raudla 2013).

Though participatory budgeting has gained increased attention in public administration literature in recent years, research in this area still remains limited (Zhang and Liao 2011) and tends to ignore its potential as a form of co-production (or, more specifically, co-planning and co-design). Indeed, public management scholars interested in this topic have mainly focused on the antecedents of participatory budgeting, the reasons leading to its adoption, the processes of implementation, the outcomes of participation.

This work is aimed at filling this gap. In particular, from the theoretical point of view, we aim at contributing to the co-production literature by providing further insights on the conditions that can lead to the successful implementation of participatory budgeting and that should be considered when looking at participatory budgeting from the perspective of co-production. From a managerial perspective, the chapter provides indications for organizations that intend to encourage citizens to co-produce public budgets and to increase the effectiveness of the process in terms of democracy, effectiveness and quality of the decision making process. More specifically, we identify four conditions of participatory budgeting that may prove helpful for successfully implementing participatory budgeting as a form of co-production: interaction, inclusiveness, responsiveness and representation.

The chapter is organized as follows. Section 3.2 briefly discusses the main features of participatory budgeting and under which conditions it can be conceived as a form of co-production, more precisely of co-planning and co-design. Section 3.3 discusses the four conditions for the successful implementation of participatory budgeting. Section 3.4 draws some conclusions.

3.2 Co-planning, Co-design and Participatory Budgeting

The phenomena concerning the engagement of individuals and community in the public service cycle have attracted increasing attention, especially in the wake of public governance movements and the recent global financial crisis. However, they have mainly focused on co-delivery, whereas much less attention has been devoted to the other facets of co-production, including co-planning and co-design that is the main object of this chapter.

In particular, co-planning and co-design refer to situations in which government and its agencies cooperate with the public (i.e., citizens, associations, interest groups, etc.) in identifying what services need to be provided to answer stakeholders' needs and in defining their characteristics. This type of involvement of non-governmental actors can take different forms and implies the use of different tools. In this chapter attention is paid to participatory budgeting.

Participatory budgeting can be seen as a form of co-planning and co-design, which entails the direct involvement of citizens on the one hand in the allocation of public resources to different public programs, services and investments and on the other in the choice of how to implement those programs and deliver those services (Bovaird 2007; Bovaird and Loeffler 2012). This is different from traditional budgeting processes where choices have usually been in the hands of elected officials, and thus citizens' choices are mediated through their representatives. On the contrary, participatory budgeting requires citizens to be directly involved in budgeting processes and responsible for decisions about budget allocations (Pinnington et al. 2009; Zhang and Yang 2009; Lerner 2011; Krenjova and Raudla 2013).

Extant literature on participatory budgeting does not generally look at participatory budgeting from the perspective of co-production, but rather describes a variety of experiences in which the degree of participation and involvement and the types of processes of participation vary widely.

As shown in Fig. 3.1, the intensity of participation of citizens in budgeting decisions may differ depending on the characteristics of the deliberation process and the distribution of responsibility between governments and citizens for the final decision. In particular, it is possible to distinguish three ladders of participation (pseudo, partial and full) (Moynihan 2007), according to which the level of co-planning and co-design varies ranging from very weak to strong.

Pseudo participation occurs when citizens only participate to open meetings, in which they mainly receive information materials from governments on priorities and available alternatives to cope with emerging problems. In some participatory budgeting processes, citizens can, for example, be invited to attend events such as

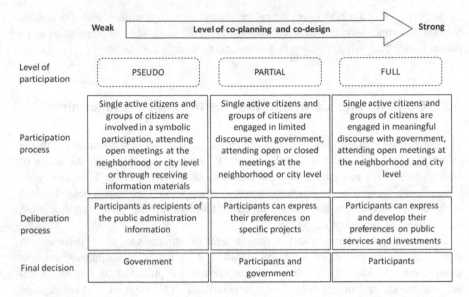

Fig. 3.1 Citizens' participation, co-planning and co-design. *Source* Elaboration from Moynihan (2007)

public hearings or community meetings. The deliberation process is characterized by the role of citizens mainly as recipients of information, whereas government autonomously takes the final decision. For these reasons, the level of co-planning and co-design is particularly weak, almost non-existent.

Partial participation implies citizens' consultation on public decision, thus with only a limited impact on public policy. For example, they may be invited to express their opinions through surveys or other tools aimed at catching their preferences on a set of pre-set alternatives (Ebdon and Franklin 2004, 2006). The fact that citizens are involved only to provide one-way comments limits their level of engagement and the possibility to influence effectively public decision. Both the participants and the government may affect the final decision, even if the government can decide to neglect the inputs received by citizens. Partial participation can be seen as characterized by a medium level of co-planning and co-design.

Finally, *full participation* occurs when citizens are massively involved in the development of the alternatives and the identification of solutions. This is the result of fruitful dialogues between the public administration and citizens and among the citizens themselves. Citizens have the chance not only to express but also to develop their preferences, which are not restricted to specific alternatives (i.e., those previously identified by the public administration) but regard public services and investments more in general. Moreover, the final decision is under the responsibility of citizens that are required to decide what to do with public money. This results in a strong level of co-planning and co-design.

In the light of the above considerations, we argue that only when the participation is full, participatory budgeting can be seen as an effective form of co-planning and co-design. This implies that adopting a co-production perspective to participatory budgeting means taking into consideration that co-planning and co-design will require the establishment, care and maintenance on the one hand of the relationship between the public administration and the citizens, and on the other the relationship among the citizens themselves. However, we also recognize that not every decision may necessarily require full participation and thus become a strong form of co-planning. Depending on the type of decision (for example, degree of controversy over it, amount of expenditure, urgency) and the context (political fragmentation and stability, level of homogeneity of citizens' preferences, etc.) different degrees of participation may be advisable or desirable. In this chapter we focus on the case of full participation in decisions related to allocation of public money.

The following section presents a framework, which, considering simultaneously the administration and the citizens' sides of participatory budgeting, identifies those conditions that allow successfully implementing the participatory budgeting as a form of co-production.

3.3 Participatory Budgeting as Co-planning and Co-design: Conditions for Success

Participatory budgeting, as a co-planning and co-design exercise, involves the establishment and nurturing of a complex web of relationships. Put simply, on the one hand it involves the relationship between the public administration and the citizens and stakeholders. On the other, it involves a web of relationships among the citizens. Under the former perspective, public administrations should ensure that all the citizens that are potentially interested in the process are included, and that continuous communication and interaction is ensured with them. Under the latter, i.e., the citizens' perspective, the participatory process must ensure both representation of the various interests and needs at stake and responsiveness to them. As previously stated, the four conditions for success that should be considered when looking at participatory budgeting from the perspective of co-production are thus *Interaction*, *Inclusiveness*, *Responsiveness* and *Representation* and are further discussed below.

3.3.1 Inclusiveness and Interaction

Inclusiveness refers to "the openness of the political system and the degree of members' participation" (Hong 2015, p. 573). It is considered a central condition for achieving democratic values and for guaranteeing a more equal allocation of resources and advancing social values (Feldman and Khademian 2007; Wampler 2007; Rossmann and Shanahan 2012). Indeed, through participatory mechanisms, traditionally excluded groups and citizens have access to decision-making venues (Shah 2007) and people can share information from different perspectives and interests (Feldman and Khademian 2007; Nabatchi 2012). Moreover, inclusiveness is also a condition to ensure a wider representation.

Both cons and pros of inclusiveness have been identified and largely debated in the literature. On the one hand, as Hong (2015) points out, greater inclusiveness may mean expanding the number of citizens involved, reducing individual sense of ownership of the process and commitment. In addition, this may increase the costs of the process (e.g., larger spaces or platforms for discussion, more information processing, longer meetings, etc. may be needed), and the need for more information, thus possibly reducing its efficiency (Moynihan 2007). Indeed, as interests that are more diverse are represented, reaching consensus may become longer and more difficult.

On the other hand, inclusiveness may enhance the deliberation process by yielding a greater number of proposals as well as resources, including knowledge and commitment (Bryson et al. 2013). Moreover, it can generate higher creativity improving the quality of the ideas discussed and of the decision taken (Hong 2015), thus positively affecting responsiveness.

Although important, inclusiveness may result difficult to achieve. Indeed, not only "women, vulnerable groups, and people living in remote areas are easily excluded" (Fölscher 2007, p. 144), but further barriers to citizens' participation also exist. The latter can depend both on the citizens' willingness to participate and/or on the ability of the government to communicate with its citizens. According to Rossmann and Shanahan (2012), the citizens' unwillingness to participate may be due to cynicism, apathy and/or to the lack of social connectedness and of technical information. For example, they may prefer to be excluded from participatory processes when they feel powerless, i.e., they think they cannot make a difference in such processes.

Governments can promote inclusiveness in the selection stage, i.e., ensuring that citizens join the process presenting projects, participating to debates and voting. From this perspective, five main criteria exist for identifying and including the actors who participate in public decision-making processes (see Fung 2006) involving:

(i)   Openness to all who wish to attend largely based on self-selection of the general population;
(ii) Selective recruitment, based on the involvement of community organizers or incentives (e.g., gift cards, transportation, meals) to ensure participation by those people who would otherwise be less likely to participate, for practical as well as motivational reasons (see also Nabatchi 2012; Nabatchi and Blomgren Amsler 2014);
(iii) Random selection of participants;

(iv) Invitation of lay stakeholders in public discussion and decision, i.e., unpaid citizens who have strong interest in specific public issues and thus are willing to participate, representing those who have similar interest but decide not to participate;

(v) Participation of professional stakeholders, i.e., representatives of organized interests or public officials.

When evaluating possible ways to select and involve citizens, one crucial decision may refer to the choice of resorting to online engagement, which may enhance efficiency, but also affect inclusion of less "digitalized" categories of citizens (Nabatchi and Blomgren Amsler 2014).

In the deliberation process, inclusiveness can be fostered in a number of ways, including availability of translation, childcare, transportation assistance (Bryson et al. 2013, p. 29) and diversity of fora for discussion (physical vs. online, diffused in different geographic areas, at different times, etc.). A typical response to the need to ensure that not only citizens are present, but also actively participate in the decisions, is the provision of information and the reliance on facilitators. Facilitators can be important in reducing or managing conflict, while at the same time ensuring that different views and voices are expressed and heard, and that virtually every participant can express her ideas in a respectful climate (Nabatchi 2012; Bryson et al. 2013).

Interaction refers to the establishment of a two-way channel of communication, continuously adjusted over time, between the public administration and its citizens.

Some scholars have argued that participation is most beneficial when characterized by a two-way communication (Ebdon and Franklin 2004) and that citizens' participation "requires dialogue and deliberation between government and citizens" (Zhang and Liao 2011, p. 284). Two-way communication is "the bidirectional flow of information, or the transfer of information wherein individuals act as both senders and receivers" (Nabatchi 2012).

While "surveys and public hearings tend to provide one-way information regarding citizen opinions" (Ebdon and Franklin 2006, p. 442) and the latter, particularly, tend to be used to "defend agency decision rather than to involve the public" in discussion (Beierle 1998, p. 21), only two-way communication may allow citizens' voices and needs to be actually taken into consideration. Thus, participatory budgeting should not be a symbolic "exercise in styles" but a process where the budget is actually "constructed" in an interactive way through a continuous and creative exchange of ideas among citizens and between the administration and the citizens. An interactive approach requires that citizens identify local problems and needs and then discuss them with politicians and civil servants in order to figure out the feasibility of projects and to find how to solve all the stumbling blocks. For example, in the experience of the Municipality of Grottamare in Italy delegates elected by citizens in each of the seven territorial districts were involved in a deliberation process and they discussed with civil servants as well as with politicians all the emerging issues and classified them in unresolved, directly resolved, district issues and municipal issues (Bassoli 2012).

Interaction may support a learning process both for citizens and for public administrations. The former are educated to play their role as co-planners because they learn about how budgeting process works and the rules, constraints and procedures related to building a new bike path or renovating a school. This learning process requires that public administrations provide citizens with information that has traditionally been available only to civil servants, increasing the degree of transparency (Wampler 2007). For example, in Porto Alegre, civil servants played a relevant role in this respect, organizing meetings, providing information to citizens about their choices, and offering technical analyses for project proposals (Moynihan 2007).

Among the mechanisms that the public administration may employ to this end, making information available to citizens seems to be an effective way to improve the quality of decisions (Nabatchi 2012; Nabatchi and Blomgren Amsler 2014). Information should be targeted to the different kind of citizens, being provided in various formats and through a variety of sources (Bryson et al. 2013). It may also be provided by the public administration organizing the participatory budgeting, or the public administration can assume a catalyst role for information, by collecting and incentivizing the circulation of proposals and projects developed by other subjects participating to the process. However, in this latter case, a problem may arise with the reliability of data and sources and the public administration may have to act as guarantor of the quality and reliability of data and to ensure that trust is built among the parties involved.

From the perspective of the public administration, through a two-way communication with citizens, governments also have access to new source of information that can lead to a better understanding of the needs of the community and to innovative ways to delivery services with an improvement of allocative or technical efficiency (Moynihan 2007). In this vein, interaction is a dimension of a co-productive approach to participatory budgeting that allows bringing together new information and new ways of understanding problems and addressing them. This takes on even more importance when budget squeezes reduce the resources at disposal and require that they be used effectively, limiting delays and mistakes.

However, interaction and its beneficial effects manifest themselves when participatory budgeting is not a one-time-only event (Nabatchi and Blomgren Amsler 2014). Nevertheless, rarely have local governments institutionalized their experiences of participatory budgeting, often relying on it only to generate an immediate return in terms of consensus on the political group that supports its implementation. To move towards a more stable and durable experience of participatory budgeting there is a need to go beyond ideological or personal reasons for its implementation and lay the conditions for its institutionalization. This requires continuity of commitment over time, irrespective of political shifts in the administration, which is facilitated if such commitment becomes credible and is embodied in physical spaces and structures (offices, meeting areas, etc.), processes and routines, as well as identifiable skills and capabilities. Through this continuity, trust can be built over time among citizens and between the citizenry and the administration, and, in turn, this will represent the needed condition for an enhanced interaction.

3.3.2   Representation and Responsiveness

Inclusiveness and interaction in the process are central in the relationship between public organizations and their citizens. However, participatory budgeting entails not only relationships between public administrations and citizens, but also *among citizens*. Thus, the final success of the participatory process will depend not only on how well the relationship between the administration and the citizens is managed, but also on how the citizens perceive their interaction among them. Moreover, the extent to which citizens feel that their own interests and needs are represented and find a suitable response are key factors for the success. Thus, responsiveness and representation are two other crucial dimensions to be taken into consideration in participatory budgeting.

Representation refers to the extent to which different interests, views and power positions have voice in the process. Perceptions that the process is not representing fairly the interests at stake may de-legitimize the process and reduce commitment (Barbera et al. 2014).

Representation requires that decisions on how to spend public money be taken mainly through open and inclusive debates. However, although being a critical element in this respect, inclusiveness of the process is not sufficient per se to ensure representation. Indeed, representation will require the choice of a way to ensure that voice and views are expressed, and of ways to avoid or reduce conflict, while selecting and compromising on possible solutions. Looking at the criteria discussed above for ensuring inclusiveness, they may produce different effects in terms of representation. While random selection method seems to be the best way to guarantee "descriptive representativeness" (Fung 2006, 68), self-selection may lead only wealthier and better-educated people to participate, or a biased representation of interests. Invitation of lay or professional stakeholders may, on the other hand, put into question their independence and representativeness and suggest that citizens remain distant from the places where decisions are taken.

As Shah (2007) observes, the more the decisions are left to a portion of the interested population, and the more appropriate mechanisms for ensuring fair representation and accountability therein are needed. A combination of inclusion systems may prove effective if there is evidence that not all the interests would be otherwise represented, for example openness to all interested citizens with additional selective recruitment or invitation of lay stakeholders. The reliance on professional stakeholders or intermediate bodies that represent groups of stakeholders will require ex-ante legitimation of such bodies, not only in terms of competencies, but also of having a sufficient base of consensus and being in continuous contact and communication with their stakeholders, to avoid their becoming self-referential.

Hopefully, a process where representation has been satisfactory will give origin to more responsive proposals. Indeed, representation is important per se, but also as it has a complex relationship with *responsiveness*, i.e., the attitude of projects presented to address and answer not only to parochial needs, but also to the collective needs and expectations.

When citizens act as co-planners they bring to the table their own perspectives, sensibilities, values and needs but, at the same time, they are required to develop a broader awareness and better understanding of the collective needs. For example, at the beginning of the process most projects and proposals may reflect parochial and distinctive needs of specific groups of people. Only when these scattered instances are translated into projects with broader scope, suited to deal with problems perceived by the community as a whole, responsiveness is achieved.

One way to address this is the institutionalization of participatory experiences. Indeed, when participatory budgeting is a stable experience, citizens become more collaborative and prone to sacrifice their particular and immediate interest for the common good and a longer-term view. This may also require mechanisms to ensure that the right balance between collective and more targeted needs (i.e., a more parochial perspective) is achieved.

In the shorter term, the selection of the projects should be the result not only of voting, but debate, whereby facilitators and the involvement of experts or professionals from the administration in the process may support the development of solutions that are largely shared, but also technically feasible and the most suitable to meet the relevant needs. When the projects are selected using voting mechanisms it seems that good results depend more on the intensive campaign made by possible beneficiaries rather than on the usefulness of the project for the community as a whole. An additional important condition for ensuring responsiveness is the availability of information, since this has been proved to enhance the quality of decisions (Nabatchi 2012). The information can be provided in traditional ways (books, papers), online, but also relying on expert involvement in presentations and discussions.

Whatever the mechanisms identified to ensure responsiveness, the rules underlying the participatory process should be made clear from the outset (Fölscher 2007). At the same time, the public administration should be strongly committed to the implementation of participatory processes and thus interaction appears to be an important condition for ensuring responsiveness. Indeed, as Ackerman (2013, p. 109) has noted, "governments can only get back as much as they put into efforts to activate civil society participation for accountability (...). Without such full involvement by the government, 'participation' schemes can easily end up only strengthening previously existing clientelistic networks and unbalanced intra-community power relations".

3.4 Conclusion

Participatory budgeting represents an important form of co-production, or, more specifically, co-planning and co-design (Bovaird 2007). This has also been addressed by some governments (i.e., UK) as well as some empirical studies. However, while in the academic domain a number of studies have looked at the reasons for its adoption, its processes and consequences, most of them have focused on the point of view of the governments, officials and politicians adopting it and have not looked at it from the perspective of co-production literature. Much less attention has been devoted to looking at the views of citizens as co-producers (or co-planners) participating in the budgetary process, thus embracing this idea coming also from outside the academia.

In this work we have argued that, though there exist different forms of participatory budgeting, if it is to be seen as a co-production form, it must satisfy four conditions for success: interaction, inclusiveness, representation and responsiveness.

Interaction and inclusiveness should shape the relationship between the public administration and its citizens, by building a virtuous two-way dialogue with citizens during the process and guaranteeing a high degree of transparency and involvement. Representation and responsiveness should become central in shaping the relationship among citizens, through the creation of mechanisms that ensure equal access to all the interests at stake while, at the same time, ensuring the quality of the final decisions, in a way that they translate into actual responses to community needs.

The chapter provides examples and reflections on how to promote greater interaction, inclusiveness, responsiveness and representation, which public administrations may find useful in successfully implementing participatory budgeting as a form of co-production. Its contribution is thus twofold.

Under a theoretical perspective, this chapter identifies the conditions for ensuring that participatory budgeting becomes a form of co-production, thus providing further support for Bovaird's (2007) argument that participatory budgeting can be useful at the planning and design stages. More specifically, a model for considering participatory budgeting as a form of co-production is proposed. Under a practical and policy perspective, it provides specific criteria and tools for increasing the level of participation in decision-making processes regarding the allocation of public money.

References

J.M. Ackerman, From co-production to co-governance, in *New Public Governance, The Third Sector, and Co-production*, ed. by V. Pestoff, T. Brandsen, B. Verschuere (Routledge, New York, 2013), pp. 101–126

G. Baiocchi, E. Ganuza, Participatory Budgeting as if emancipation mattered. Polit. Soc. **42**(1), 29–50 (2014). doi:10.1177/0032329213512978

C. Barbera, M. Sicilia, I. Steccolini, What Mr Rossi wants in participatory budgeting: two Rs (Responsiveness and Representation) and two Is (Interaction and Inclusiveness), in *Paper Presented at the IIAS Study Group on 'Coproduction of Public Services'*, 20–21 May 2014, Bergamo (Italy), (2014)

M. Bassoli, Participatory budgeting in Italy: An analysis of (almost democratic) participatory governance arrangements. Int. J. Urban Regional **36**(6), 1183–1203 (2012). doi:10.1111/j.1468-2427.2011.01023.x

T.C. Beierle, *Public Participation in Environmental Decisions: An Evaluation Framework Using Social Goals* (Resources for the Future, Washington, DC, 1998)

T. Bovaird, Beyond Engagement and Participation: User and Community Coproduction of Public Services. Public Admin. Rev. **67**(5), 846–860 (2007). doi:10.1111/j.1540-6210.2007.00773.x

T. Bovaird, E. Loeffler, From engagement to co-production: How users and communities contribute to public services, in *New Public Governance, The Third Sector, and Co-production*, ed. by V. Pestoff, T. Brandsen, B. Verschuere (Routledge, New York, 2012), pp. 35–60

J.M. Bryson, K.S. Quick, C.S. Slotterback, B.C. Crosby, Designing public participation processes. Public Adm. Rev. **73**(1), 23–34 (2013). doi:10.1111/j.1540-6210.2012.02678.x

C. Ebdon, A. Franklin, Searching for a role for citizens in the budget process. Public Budg. Finance **24**(1), 32–49 (2004). doi:10.1111/j.0275-1100.2004.02401002.x

C. Ebdon, A. Franklin, Citizen participation in budgeting theory. Public Adm. Rev. **66**(3), 437–447 (2006). doi:10.1111/j.1540-6210.2006.00600.x

M.S. Feldman, A.M. Khademian, The role of the public manager in inclusion: Creating communities of participation. Governance **20**(2), 305–324 (2007). doi:10.1111/j.1468-0491.2007.00358.x

A. Fölscher, Participatory budgeting in central and Eastern Europe, in ed. by A. Shah Participatory budgeting (The World Bank 2007), pp. 127–156

A. Fung, Varieties of participation in complex governance. Public Adm. Rev. **66**(s1), 66–75 (2006). doi:10.1111/j.1540-6210.2006.00667.x

S. Hong, Citizen participation in budgeting: A trade-off between knowledge and inclusiveness? Public Adm. Rev. **75**(4), 572–582 (2015). doi:10.1111/puar.12377

J. Krenjova, R. Raudla, Participatory budgeting at the local level: challenges and opportunities for new democracies. Adm. Cult. **14**(1), 18–46 (2013)

J. Lerner, Participatory budgeting: Building community agreement around tough budget decisions. Natl. Civic Rev. **100**(2), 30–35 (2011). doi:10.1002/ncr.20059

D.P. Moynihan, Citizen participation in budgeting: Prospects for developing countries, in *Participatory Budgeting*, ed. by A. Shan (The World Bank, Washington DC, 2007), pp. 21–54

T. Nabatchi, Putting the "Public" back in public values research: Designing, participation to identify and respond to values. Public Adm. Rev. **72**(5), 699–708 (2012). doi:10.1111/j.1540-6210.2012.02544.x

T. Nabatchi, L. Blomgren Amsler, Direct public engagement in local government. Am. Rev. Public Adm. **44**(4S), 63S–88S (2014). doi:10.1177/0275074013519702

E. Pinnington, J. Lerner, D. Schugurensky, Participatory budgeting in North America: The case of Guelph, Canada. J. Public Budg. Account. Financ. Manage. **21**(3), 454–463 (2009)

C. Pollitt, G. Bouckaert, E. Löffler, *Making Quality Sustainable: Co-design, Co-decide, Co-produce and Co-Evaluate* (Ministry of Finance, Helsinki, 2006)

D. Rossmann, E.A. Shanahan, Defining and achieving normative democratic values in participatory budgeting processes. Public Adm. Rev. **72**(1), 56–66 (2012). doi:10.1111/j.1540-6210.2011.02480.x

A. Shah, Overview, in *Participatory Budgeting*, ed. by A. Shah (The World Bank 2007)

M. Sicilia, E. Guarini, A. Sancino, M. Andreani, R. Ruffini, Public service management and co-production in multi-level governance settings. Int. Rev. Adm. Sci., Published on-line on June 5, 2015 (2015). doi:10.1177/0020852314566008

Y. Sintomer, C. Herzberg, A. Röcke, Participatory budgeting in Europe: Potentials and challenges. Int. J. Urban Reg **2**(1), 164–178 (2008). doi:10.1111/j.1468-2427.2008.00777.x

I. Steccolini, Is the annual report an accountability medium? An empirical investigation into Italian local governments. Financ. Account. Manage. **20**(3), 327–350 (2004)

B. Wampler, A guide to participatory budgeting, in *Participatory Budgeting*, ed. by A. Shan (The World Bank, Washington DC, 2007), pp. 21–54

Y.H. Zhang, K. Yang, Citizen participation in the budget process: The effect of city managers. J. Public Budg. Account. Financ. Manage. **21**(2), 289–317 (2009). ISSN: 1096-3367

Y.H. Zhang, Y. Liao, Participatory budgeting in local government. Evidence from New Jersey municipalities. *Public Perform*. Manag. Rev. **35**(2), 281–302 (2011). doi:10.2753/PMR1530-9576350203

Chapter 4
When is Personalisation Considered a Form of Co-production? The Case of Personal Budgets Reform in English Social Care

Enrico Bracci and Danny Chow

4.1 Introduction

In recent times, co-production has become an all-embracing term applied in different contexts and with several meanings. Broadly speaking, co-production can be considered any "regular, long-term relationships between professionalized service providers and service users" (Bovaird 2007, p. 847). Osborne and Strokosch (2013) differentiated co-production into three categories: operational, strategy and service. Although some of these categories may overlap, the focus of the present chapter is on the operational model of co-production.

In particular, this chapter considers how the personalisation policy of social care in England was translated in practice and if it can be considered a form of co-production. In the mid-2000s, Individual Budgets (IB), and its related programme Personal Budgets (PB), represented a suite of reform programmes underpinned by accounting-centric notions of personalised co-production of public services. These programmes, with PB at the centre, reflected the government's drive to transform public services through personalisation. The basic rationale is that by giving 'clients' (users of public services in receipt of social support) control over the money used to fund their social care, it is implicitly assumed that this will facilitate the alignment between the care received and the clients' needs and preferences (Duffy 2007).

Although this chapter is the joint effort of both authors, the sections can be attributed as follows: Sects. 4.1, 4.2, 4.3 and 4.6 to Enrico Bracci, Sects. 4.4 and 4.5 to Danny Chow.

E. Bracci (✉)
University of Ferrara, Ferrara, Italy
e-mail: enrico.bracci@unife.it

D. Chow
Durham University, Durham, UK

© The Author(s) 2016   41
M. Fugini et al. (eds.), *Co-production in the Public Sector*,
PoliMI SpringerBriefs, DOI 10.1007/978-3-319-30558-5_4

In contrast, the traditional approach to social care delivery relied on services delivered by local authorities (LAs) within a public administration paradigm (Osborne 2006). Under this approach (which is still practiced in many LAs), social care managers were solely responsible for assigning services to clients. The introduction of PB was intended to encourage LAs to adopt more flexible and creative ways of providing social care through the joint and pro-active involvement of service users (Wilberforce et al. 2011). Under PB, the care budget is devolved to the user, based on the level of need. The responsibility to assign a personal budget to the customised services/goods is placed at the user level through the mediating role of care manager (Needham 2011).

The PB concept is thus more in line with recent innovations in public service delivery, which extends beyond traditional service planning and management towards the co-production of public services (Fotaki 2009). The introduction of personalisation in social care affects the overall governance of power and responsibility, specifically from central government to LAs, and from care managers to service users (Duffy 2007). An attempt at conceptualising the trend of personalisation in social care then is to view it as an operational form of co-production (Osborne and Strokosch 2013). From this perspective, the service user is expected to engage with, and is engaged by, professionals in the design of the service. The dynamics of the engagement is then said to empower the service user, aligning expectations with their experience of service delivery. The on-going debate is on whether personalisation as a concept, and the personal budget as a core technology, can be construed as a type of co-production. This chapter aims to address this unresolved issue of definition.

The rest of the chapter is structured as follows: Sects. 4.2 and 4.3 review the literature on co-production in social care. Section 4.4 is a description of reforms centred on personalisation in England and its main features. Section 4.5 describes the structure and use of personalisation process and a personal budget, and presents the analysis of personalisation and co-production as a shared responsibility. Section 4.6 concludes the chapter.

4.2   Co-production in Social Care: Literature Review

In public services, and in social care services in particular, the active participation of and inputs from users have always been considered key determinants of effective outcomes. Users of social services already make contributions at the different stage of the process: from assessment to planning, from commissioning to implementation and so forth (Hunter and Ritchie 2007). However, the concept of co-production, despite being first mooted in the 1970s, faded away and fell into disused in the 1980s. The main reason was the increasing popularity of New Public Management (NPM) then, in which rational concepts of reorganising the public sector (embodied in ideas such as efficiency and effectiveness) and the wider use of quasi-market tools (e.g., competitive tendering and vouchers) envisaged users as individual consumers.

In social care, co-production then was marginalised by two competing organising philosophies of welfarism-professionalism and consumerism-managerialism (Pestoff 2009). Welfarism and professionalism conceived of a strong role for the State in designing, planning implementing and reviewing the social services, leaving no room for users' involvement. On the other end of the scale, consumerism promoted the creation of market mechanisms with users behaving as customers. As a consequence, users who are unsatisfied with services received are expected to rely mainly on exit mechanisms (like the notional consumer) by choosing a different provider available in the market. In such situations, co-production was not considered as a solution to improve efficiency and effectiveness of the social services.

However, the failure of reform programmes operating under the NPM banner to deliver all of its promises has led to the revival of co-production as a principle for the reorganisation of public services. Perceived inadequacies of NPM has also led academics to shift towards a New Public Governance (NPG) mode (Osborne and Strokosch 2013; Osborne 2006). As previously noted, the genesis of co-production is not new. In the 1990s, some scholars have suggested that the management of social care should replace managerial theories derived from the manufacturing industry with the co-production framework (Wilson 1994).

The return of co-production in debates around the management and organisation of social care discussion can be attributed to the following reasons (Needham et al. 2012, pp. 2–3):

- A reduced faith in target-based and market process.
- An increased call for devolution of power up to the users/citizens.
- A pressure to increase efficiency and reduce public spending.
- The growing awareness of the importance of the knowledge generated via the user interaction.
- An increased determination to make social care more personal, increasing the effective participation of users.

As a delivery mechanism for social care services, co-production is not new, given that the interaction between users and social workers has always been critical to achieving a successful outcome. However, the ways in which co-production may take place can be several and with different characteristics. Needham et al. (2012, pp. 9–10) suggested at least three types of co-production in social care:

(1) *Compliant (or descriptive) co-production*: this is the most basic form of co-production. Social services can only be delivered if the user takes part in the process. The process can highlight compliant of procedures without the necessary deep engagement in bringing about meaningful change. Under this form of co-production, the service provider and the user agree on the definition of the problem, and the design and implementation of the possible solution. This type of engagement is not set up to significantly change users' lives.

(2) *Supportive (or intermediate) co-production*: this form involves wider recognition of the diversity and importance of roles around the user. More responsibilities are given to the users in defining outcomes and in direct problem solving of complex issues.

(3) *Transformative co-production*: it has the potential to create additional relationships between the users and social workers that support them. Users are given a more pro-active role in shaping the services and the social workers alike. At this stage, all opportunities given by co-production are exploited and social care becomes more attentive to the variation in needs of individuals and to the wider context of social care.

Indeed, co-production in social care aims to have a transformative role, affecting not only the provision of public services, but also users' lives (Realpe and Wallace 2010). It recognises the active role and contribution in the successful delivery of social care, while at the same time the empowerment of social workers when dealing with the users. Wilson (1994) explains that the extent to which social care can be co-produced depends on several issues:

(a) *Normative*: laws and regulations may define some limitations and/or obligations in the use of forms of co-production. This may be due to the risk involved (i.e., mental illness), or the need to control funding.

(b) *Ethical*: co-production may involve choices considered valuable for the user but not necessarily for society as a whole. Consider, for instance, the case of a user buying a seasonal football ticket to increase his or her autonomy and assimilation with other members of the society—Would this be universally considered social care? Questions can also be raised as to its appropriateness as a use of public funds.

(c) *Equity*: co-producing means also to design and implement services specifically tailored for a single user or a small group. Such a situation may lead to unfair differentiation and access to resources.

(d) *Technical*: co-production requires adequate staff in both quantity and expertise, as it can be time-consuming and challenging to implement, mainly because staff expertise has to be built through training and experience.

(e) *Organisational*: co-production may challenge the efficacy of existing systems of service delivery and threaten the organisational hierarchy. Existing modes of public sector operations are seen to be less efficient and more paternalistic compared to co-production, leaving them vulnerable to downsizing or even to closure.

(f) *Financial*: co-production requires an additional and secure source of funding in order to sustain the process, alongside current spending on social care, which could be challenging in austere periods for the public sector.

It is not surprising that the Social Care Institute for Excellence (2013) foresaw four areas of change needed in order to implement a co-production model in social care:

- *Culture*: in terms of individual and/or organisational beliefs, values and principles at work.
- *Structure*: the organisational patterns, the way resources are allocated.
- *Practice*: the way co-production is carried out by the organisation, in terms of processes and technologies used.
- *Review*: controlling and evaluating the results achieved and learning how to improve what went wrong.

There are many scenarios where co-production is an appropriate mode of social care delivery. Co-production can be used with different people in disparate social contexts and conditions. Co-production can benefit from the users' knowledge in creating value and improving the services and foster the development of peer-support mechanism between users. Through the continuous interaction between the actors involved, new knowledge is then created and new outcomes for public services will be defined, potentially leading to improvements in value for money. Overall, co-production could nurture the development of social capital in the community, through networking and self-support among individuals and associations.

In the context of social care, it is important to distinguish between different types of services under co-production, ranging from long-term care to short-term interventions. In the former case, like care for the elderly and the frail people, users and social workers are formally linked to each other for extended periods, for which voice is the only governance option if users are disgruntled with the service received. The salience—meaning the scale of relative importance of the services to the individual user—of this type of services is high and co-production may support the creation of public value. The concept of public value has many definitions and proposals and has been equated with many things, however using Moore (1995) public value can be defined as: "A framework that helps us connect what we believe is valuable and requires public resources, with improved ways of understanding what our 'publics' value and how we connect to them".

At the other extreme, the second case of short-term services, such as home-based care, allows users to exercise exit strategies in case of complaints over the quantity and quality of services. Pestoff (2012), in combining the salience of social services and the ease of involvement of users, proposed a two-by-two matrix (Table 4.1) to frame co-production opportunities.

It is not surprising that access to participation is key to determining the opportunities for co-production, with users being able to transit from passive client to active consumer. The extent to which involvement is possible depends not only

Table 4.1 Citizen involvement in social service co-production

Salience	Accessibility and engagement	
	Low	High
Greater	Active consumer	Active co-producer
Less	Passive client	Ad hoc participant

Source Adapted from Pestoff (2012, p. 25)

on the type of services, but mainly on the regulatory conditions and the organisational choices made by each public sector organisation. As Pestoff (2012) stressed, both NPM and traditional public administration logics tend to reduce access to participation, with the former advocating a consumerist approach that actively exercises choice amongst a variety of service providers, whilst the latter mandating users passively receive services assigned to them.

4.3 Conceptualising Co-production

The previous sections and the introductory chapter earlier in this book have illustrated some of the complexity and challenges in trying to define and conceptualise what co-production is or is not. We draw on Pestoff's proposed concepts, which argue that the salience, or importance of a particular service to the user, and the accessibility and engagement of the service with the user, forms the basis for understanding the relationship between personalisation and co-production. This is also Brandsen and Honingh's (2015) starting point, which overlaps with Pestoff's concepts. Brandsen and Honingh (2015) considered two main variables:

(1) The degree of involvement of users both at the design and implementation stage;
(2) The closeness between the core service of the public service organisation and the tasks performed by the users.

In combining the above variables, four possible case-situations are possible:

- *Complementary co-production in service design and implementation.* When users perform tasks that are complementary to those of the public service organisation, but co-produce both the design and implementation. As an example, an elderly group organising cultural activities at the local museum. In such cases, users are not involved in the core activities of the organisation.
- *Complementary co-production in implementation.* In this situation, users are not involved in the design of complementary activities, but co-produce the actual implementation. As an example, handicapped users helping social workers in preparing a theatrical production.
- *Co-production in the design and implementation of core-services.* It occurs when users are involved in both the design and implementation of activities representing the core mission of the organisation. As an example, a user with mental health issues defining the psychological and/or behavioural improvements and the activities to be implemented in order to achieve them.
- *Co-production in the implementation of core services.* It occurs when users are involved not in the design, but only in the implementation of the organisation's core activities. In such activities, users' involvement and participation in the implementation phase are crucial for outcomes, but these are framed within the context of professionally determined solutions.

4.4　Personalisation Agenda in England and Co-production

The etymology of 'personalisation', as applied to public services, is as ambiguous as co-production itself. It is often used in relation to different things and describing different policy decisions. Personalisation is sometimes linked to the transference of risk and responsibilities to the users, or as a new mode of engaging users.

In England, the debate on personalisation can be dated back to the beginning of the new century, within the modernisation manifesto of the Labour Government (Ferguson 2007; Gardner 2011; Glendinning 2008). Social movements such as "In Control" and "Independent Living" provided the initial drive to improve social care and social work through personalisation initiatives (Duffy 2007; Leadbeater 2004). Table 4.2 summarises the main policy documents that were produced to implement personalisation as a new mode of planning, designing, delivering and assessing social care, but also healthcare and education. From the 2006 white paper "Our health, our care, our say: a new direction for community services", to the 2011 Think Local Act Personal (TLAP) agreement, the discussion in England was centred on how social care can be personalised in order to meet wider public sector objectives using resources more efficiently and improving the care outcomes.

Personalisation is a social care approach described by the Department of Health as meaning that "Giving people greater choice and control over the services they use, we also need to ensure that everyone in society has a voice that is heard. When people get involved and use their voice they can shape improvements in provision and contribute to greater fairness in service use" (Department of Health 2006, p. 165). Personalisation is primarily a way of thinking about services and those who

Table 4.2 The personalisation policy in England: a retrospective view

Year	Act/document	Content
2006	White paper "Our health, our care, our say: a new direction for community services"	Users should have a bigger voice over the care they receive Introduced the individual budget as the means to achieve personalisation
2007	White paper "Putting people first"	Increased choice and control in adult social care, focusing in prevention, enablement and high quality of personally tailored services
2010	White paper "Equity and Excellence"	Strengthened the potential of personal budgets to improve outcomes
2010	DH paper "A vision for Social Care"	Confirmed a greater rollout of personal budgets and direct payments to increase choice and control Stresses the role of community action to increase the social capital
2011	Think Local, Act Personal (TLAP)	Sector led approach to improving personalisation and building community capacity

use them, rather than being a worked out set of policy prescriptions. Carr (2010, p. 67) argued how personalisation requires 'thinking about public services in an entirely different way—starting with the person rather than the service'. It also encompasses the provision of improved information and advice on care and support for families, investment in preventive services to reduce or delay people's need for care and the promotion of independence and self-reliance among individuals and communities (Carr and Robbins 2009).

Such policies subsequently formed part of a broader debate that has linked public service reform more generally with the role of the citizen, 'co-production' processes, and a 'double devolution' of power away from state bureaucrats towards LAs, and to frontline professionals and end-users (Needham 2011). Power and responsibility to choose the service is shared between users and providers, within the budget and the care plan assigned by the professionals (Bracci 2014). In this sense, the user co-designs and co-produces a personalised type of care, based on his/her needs. Professionals, under this scheme, supervise and control the outputs and outcomes achieved through the care received.

The outcomes/consequences of the personalization agenda are still under debate and show a mixed picture. Some research showed that early PB adopters experienced improved autonomy and control over their daily lives (Glendinning et al. 2008). Others outlined negative consequences in terms of diluted public accountability when risks and responsibilities are devolved (Bovaird 2007), and/or the de-professionalization of social care that marginalizes the role of social workers (Ellis 2015).

Despite the criticisms, PB is in line with the overall tendency to go beyond the traditional conception of service planning and management, "where public officials are exclusively charged with the responsibility for designing and providing services to citizens, who in turn only demand, consumes and evaluate them" (Pestoff 2006, p. 506), towards more co-production of public services. However, it is important to differentiate between the delivery mechanism (the budget), and the approach (personalised care, person-centred support). For example, the process of assigning a budget to a user is not co-production per se, but it may become co-production in relation to the support methods adopted, the social networks built and the overall availability of quality services in the market.

Indeed, co-production does not only involve the choice of the provider of a service, but also the co-planning and co-delivery of what is ought to satisfy the user's need (Pestoff et al. 2006; Pestoff 2006). Pestoff (2006) argued that co-production qualifies when a mix of activities occurs involving both public services agents and citizens to the provision of public services. Co-production refers to the active involvement and empowerment of users, as well as the community as a whole, in designing, delivering and consuming public services (Brudney and England 1983). In this sense, personalisation means a move from "one best way" of doing things to a repertoire of possible choices. Individual personalisation is considered particularly relevant in case of so called "soft" public services (Brudney and England 1983) like education as well as welfare services. In particular, within the different patterns in which co-production can occur, reference is made to the concept of consumer co-production (Osborne and Strokosch 2013). In a consumer co-production type, the aim is to empower users by engaging them at the operational stage of service production in order to balance expectations and experience of the service (Osborne and Strokosch 2013).

4.5 Personalisation and Co-production as a Shared Responsibility

Personalisation and personal budgets are, thus, two distinct but linked features of social care provision in England. Although the up-take of PB in 2013 involved some 30 % of all eligible users, the government is committed to widening the reach and scope of personalisation. The changes, compared to the previous systems, are numerous, particularly in terms of distribution of responsibility and accountability. In fact, a concern raised by the introduction of co-production is the potential dilution of public accountability (Bovaird 2007). Indeed, personalisation of social care involves the devolution of responsibility and power down the line to the individual user (often referred to as the 'client' by our interviewees at the local authority). This user/client is now being institutionally reconstituted as an 'accountable' person (Bracci 2014).

Table 4.3 summarises the main changes brought about by the introduction of personal budget in particular.

Users become responsible not just for the use of money available, but most of all for the choice and design of the services in order to achieve the desired outcome. By agreeing to manage a personal budget, the user become accountable for its use and the results achieved. Higher up the organisational chain, care managers share responsibility for the design of services needed within the mechanism of the users' support plan. The expectation is that users who are also PB holders and their care managers should be involved in a continuous process of dialogue in order to shape the most suitable choice of services that can fulfil the expected outcomes.

It is important to note that whilst the role of social workers is not being diminished with the advent of PB, there is a recognition of the significant shifts in skills required to deliver and manage social care, which ranges from emotional labour, implementing statutory mandates, to financial planning and management. For example, social workers are now expected, as part of the wider redefinition of care delivery under PB, to be aware of the need to manage well the mix between budget finances and service procurement. Carr (2010) identified the new skills needed as being the following:

- Decision-making—helping service users decide whether a direct payment or council-managed personal budget is right for them.
- Needs assessment and resource allocation—assessing service users' needs, or supporting them to assess their own needs, and allocating a budget to meet them, based on a resource allocation system.

Table 4.3 Responsibility and accountability changes through PB

Actor	Before PB	Under PB
Clients	Limited or absent responsibility for the choice of the services	Responsible for the choice of the services and the outcomes to be achieved (Support Plan)
	Not relevant or accountable on the use of money (if direct payment)	Accountable on the use of money and the outcome achieved
Care managers	Responsible for the type of services provided to clients	Co-responsible for the choice of the services and the outcomes to be achieved (Support Plan)
	Accountable for achieving financial target and performance measures (star systems)	Accountable on the use of money and the outcome achieved, as well as other performance measures (star system)
Local authority	Responsible for the provision of services and the financial targets	Responsible for the creation of the market place (commissioning) and the achievement of performance targets on IB and financial targets
	Accountable under the performance assessment and indicators	Accountable under the performance assessment and indicators

Source Bracci (2014)

- Reviewing the size of a personal budget—in case that a person's personal budget is insufficient to meet his/her needs, the social worker would take the case to a LA funding panel.
- Support planning and brokerage—drawing up a support plan in partnership with the service user and their family, and brokerage, i.e., providing information on or sourcing services to implement the support plan (see Fig. 4.2 as an example).

The complexity of the tasks resulting from a shift to PB implies that the personalisation of social care in England is more constitutive of a process involving not just socio-psychological needs assessments, but also financial budgeting and managerial skills in managing the out-sourced procurement of services. Figure 4.1, based on our observations of PB implementation at an anonymous English local authority, sketches the main phases of a personalised care within this processual outlook. The case organization is a medium size local authority in a large conurbation in northern England that provides a whole range of social care services, such as elderly home and residential care, adult social care and child social care.

Within the PB scheme, the work of social workers starts with the contact assessment, during which the user asks for support for his/her own needs. The process makes it clear that personalisation is embedded within the system from the very beginning. Users are required to fill a Needs Assessment Questionnaire (NAQ), or a Resource Allocation System (RAS) as it is called in some other LAs, which is designed to individually configure the requirements of users. The self-assessment data, in simple cases, leads to the quantification of the indicative budget allowed to the user. In more complex cases, the NAQ is then fed to an expert panel, composed by social workers, responsible for setting an indicative budget

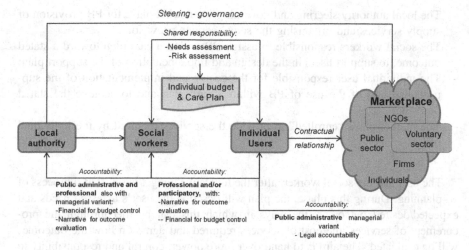

Fig. 4.1 Personalisation: the responsibility/accountability relations in the new governance

based on an assessment of the level of support needed, which is further mediated by the social worker's professional evaluations. In this phase, the expert group can focus on the level of risk involved (for instance if the eligible user has a drug addiction problem), or on other issues which requires a specific assessment. Before a user is eligible to manage their own PB, he/she is further assessed for the potential risk of abuse, safety and freedom from harm and discrimination.

Upon conclusion of the assessment, users will then be notified of their eligibility for a PB as well as the indicative budget awarded. Subsequent to approval, the user, in collaboration with the care manager, sets out to develop a personal support plan, describing the way the money will be spent and the outcomes to be achieved. In this phase the user, together with the social worker, has to estimate the cost of the services he/she would like to buy with the PB. The support plan will periodically be subjected to scrutiny of actual monies used and outcomes achieved. This happens when the support plan is referred to the Board and Administration (B&A) of the local authority. As an example, the NAQ (or RAS) is intended to give users some level of power, control and responsibility over their needs.

The support plan and the outcome matrix represented important technologies that had a dual use—planning and control on the one hand and financial accountability on the other (Bracci 2014). This reveals a process of sharing/delegating responsibility between the local authority and the user. The number of actors involved in the delivery of PB expands as the need of governing and coordinating mechanisms increases. In a governance network, the relations can be interpreted in terms of the vertical and horizontal nature of relationships between actors. In particular, it is relevant to assert "to whom" and "from who" and by "which means" accountability is being rendered (Bardach and Lesser 1996).

As depicted in Fig. 4.1, the actors involved in the process of governing and delivering PBs are the followings:

- The local authority steering and governing the market place for PB provision of supply services and organising the social service provision;
- The social workers responsible to assign PB within a care plan toward a stated outcome, to support users in the design and implementation of the support plan;
- The individual user responsible for the design and implementation of the support plan and of the use of PB within a care plan and to achieve the stated outcome;
- The market place "enrolled" to provide the services required by the individual user.

The user and the social worker, after the indicative budget is set, start a process of co-planning. During this phase, the plan will describe the user's assessed needs and expected/desired outcomes, the ways in which this can be met through the procurement of services, the cost of services required and agree on how the outcomes will be evaluated. The aim is to hand over more power, control and responsibility to the user (Bovaird 2007). Indeed, under PBs the user is left free to choose, for example, what type of care and how often to receive the support, within the total amount assigned and the care plan arranged. This process can appear creative in some cases, as user involvement means that original and sometimes even unusual approaches to working out care solutions are not uncommon. There are safeguards to the amount of creativity allowed, as ultimately social workers will have to vet PB plans and service delivery. In this respect, PB is more than a change in the way social care is delivered; it is also a cultural change both for professionals and for users.

In Fig. 4.2, the policy of the (anonymous) local authority observed is to empower users by giving them the freedom to come up with their ideas about how to spend the PBs, rather than imposing a schedule of 'allowable choices'. From the LA's perspective, the control is to be explicit upfront over activities and/or services that are disallowed, but otherwise granting freedom and trust to the user to choose the service most relevant. Once the support plan (also called *care plan*) has been drawn up, it is subjected to scrutiny by an internal panel made up of care managers and other social workers. Subsequent to the approval of the plan, the social worker and user share joint responsibility for its implementation and other associated risks.

Personalisation therefore differs notably from traditional means of delivering public services, where the full responsibility and risk over the choices made to satisfy the citizens' needs are borne by the government alone (Pestoff 2006). In the context of PBs, the active participation of users is intended, by design, to reduce the government and professionals' responsibilities (Ackerman 2004) by devolving part of the risks of decisions made and day-to-day management to the user. This shift of responsibilities through joint determination is differentiated from a NPM-oriented approach, in which users are given money to "buy" the services available from the marketplace.

Figure 4.2 illustrates a typical support plan. As previously explained, a user, with the support of the social workers, would set out the type of support he/she thinks will need. Time and other expenses are also quantified. The budget is given

	SWIFT No:
	Date Plan Developed/Updated: 15/06/09
Name: **Address:** 1 Any Street, Any Town	

MY SUPPORT PLAN

I would like my mum to support me with longer trips and the trips abroad. My mum will help me to decide what activities it would be safe for me to do on my own and when I will need support. She will help me to understand the risks and what I can do to keep safe.	
How do you want to spend your personal budget? I would like my entire personal budget to be a direct payment and for my mum to help me with this. I will use the direct payment to pay for: Personal assistants to support me with going out. (Social Inclusion and respite for carer.) Train travel and Youth Hostels in Europe. (Social inclusion and respite for carer) Personal Budget per annum = £12,146.89 One off upfront payment = £2542.49 £134.40 Insurance £167.09 Contingency £2000 Annual to cover respite/holidays £241.00 Annual subscription for Caravan club, National Trust, English Heritage, North Bay Railway, Piano Examination fee Weekly payment = £184.70 (equivalent £9604.40 annually) 9 hours of Personal Assistant support per week @ £9.50 per hour = £85.50 Day activities = £71.20 (can be used for additional PA hours if required) £28.00 for travel per week	Think about – What support will you be paying for and what will not be paid for? Do you want your social care worker to arrange services for you, or do you want a direct or indirect payment, or do you want a combination of both? How much will your support cost?

Fig. 4.2 The individual support plan: extract

directly to the user, or to a broker appointed by the user or managed as a virtual budget by a social worker. In the first case, the user is required to account for the actual use of the money and, through an annual review, to evaluate the outcomes achieved. The support plan, as illustrated in Fig. 4.2, used plain English that is free of any technical jargon, in order to ensure that users are comfortable with the process, regardless of their language and communication skills.

The support plan is a technology designed to actively engage the user into a reflective dialogue with his/her social worker through the construction of objectives, action points, timelines and budget allocations. The support plan in Fig. 4.2 exemplifies how co-production could materialise within a Personal Budget scheme, as the user together with his/her social worker iteratively revise the support plan until they come to an agreement. The process of co-production ends when the care/support plan is approved and allocated a budget. The next stage of the personalisation process, which extends beyond co-production, is the implementation phase of the designed service and of the accountability process. In presenting the support plan, the user takes full responsibility over the way public money is to be spent and for what purpose. Users are made aware that, in case of abuse (e.g., unauthorised used of funds), the PB will be suspended indefinitely. The social worker also shares responsibility in signing off the PB support plan.

Co-production, and, therefore, trust between social workers and users are based on co-decision and co-planning of the support plan. Whilst ironically some social workers compared this joint decision making process to traditional paternalistic roles of social services under the welfarism-professionalism mode, a key differentiator is that user self-determination is at the very heart of social work practice. This notion of self-determination supports the claim that personalisation is a return to 'true' social work, through the nurturing of vulnerable or marginalised users' independence and the wider societal inclusion that managing a budget and being in charge of one's own treatment can bring (Leadbeater 2004). However, there are no guarantees that the personalisation process and the personal budget will lead to more substantive engagement between users to co-produce the service. The low level of PB uptake, when compared with the Government's target, suggests that there is still a way to go before the full-expected benefits of cultural and policy change can be realised.

4.6   Discussion and Final Reflections

The aim of this chapter was to understand the policy-oriented shift towards personalisation in social care, and address the issue of whether personalisation can be considered a type of co-production. It is important to separate the concept of personalisation from the process of applying personal budgets to adult social care in England. While the latter can be considered the means through which personalisation happens, the former is the rationalisation to make care more tailored to the individual. In other words, personalisation is a process of designing and implementing a social care plan, which is then put into practice using instruments such as PBs.

In order to establish whether the personalisation of care through the use of PB can be considered a means of co-production, users need to be supported by public organisations to develop the social networks necessary to support co-production. Users must be given an active role, pooling their resources with those of the public and social workers.

As Table 4.4 stresses, personalisation may only be considered as co-production if it is implemented within a citizenship model oriented to social justice and inclusion. If personalisation is reduced simply to the transfer of money and responsibility to purchase services in the open market, the joint decision making process that underpins co-production would cease to exist. In such situations, local authorities are thus relegated to the role of gatekeepers, responsible only for assessing PB eligibility and maintaining a market place for users to purchase services required. This would not be co-production, but instead represent a consumerist view of social care with a passive role for the users and where public sector organisations are absolved of joint responsibility for the decision, provision and active management of care delivery.

It is clear that personalisation cannot deliver co-production in every single case, since co-production involves an active role by both parties and the pooling of resources. As some research on the evaluation of PB showed (Hatton and Waters 2013), users may not even know how their PB are being used, and/or don't have the proper information and knowledge on how to use it. At the institutional level, some authors argued that the implementation of PB by local authorities can be seen as a cynical way to devolve risk and responsibilities to budget holders (Ferguson 2007; Junne and Huber 2014), especially during periods of austerity with decreasing levels of public funding (Bracci and Chow 2015).

In reflecting back on the conceptual framework, personalisation can potentially be considered as a non-complementary form of co-production in the design and in the implementation of core and no-core service. Under PB, the process of constructing the support plan can lead to the design of a core service, pooling knowledge and resources from both sides. At the same time, the actual implementation of core services designed through the support plan could conceive of a more active and involved role for users and carers working towards mutually agreed

Table 4.4 Citizenship model and co-production

Social justice and inclusion	Consumerist
Family/friend/partner/relationships	Cash for care
Neighbourliness	Shop for care
Looking out for each other	Marketplace principles
Social capacity and capital	Trading standards
Co-production	Buyer beware
Inclusivity of community activities and services	Citizen/social networking/user posed information
Outreach	
Regulation or accreditation	

Source Adapted from I&DeA (2009, p. 43)

outcomes. In this process, additional non-core services can be considered in both the design and the implementation of core services.

Personalisation can, thus, be considered as a co-production only if the relationship between the social worker and user starts from the design and following implementation of both core and non-core complementary services. Plans devised solely by local authority and/or the social workers at the implementation stage cannot be considered personalised care.

Overall, personalisation, by its very nature, entails the design and the implementation of care involving substantive input from all actors within the wider community. Only when this condition is met can personalisation be considered a form of co-production and be in a position to deliver the claimed benefits in terms of value for money. Such a view is consistent with Duffy's (2007), in that there is no guarantee that every individual PB programme will involve co-production. The latter can be considered as a desired aim of personalisation, but it should not be taken for granted. Only if the essential elements described above are present, real co-production is possible; otherwise personalisation is a façade for other political agendas both at the central and local government level. These socio-political dynamics are understudied, and needs to be taken into considerations by scholars both from a public management and accounting perspective in future research on the development of personalisation in social care.

References

J. Ackerman, Co-governance for accountability: beyond "exit" and "voice". World Dev. **32**, 447–463 (2004). doi:10.1016/j.worlddev.2003.06.015

E. Bardach, C. Lesser, Accountability in human services collaboratives-for what? and to whom? J. Public Adm. Res. Theory **6**, 197–224 (1996). doi:10.1093/oxfordjournals.jpart.a024307

T. Bovaird, Beyond engagement and participation: user and community co-production of public services. Public Adm. Rev. **67**, 846–860 (2007)

E. Bracci, Accountability and governance in social care: the impact of personalisation. Qual. Res. Account. Manag. **11**, 111–128 (2014)

E. Bracci, D.S.L. Chow, Personalised adult social care in England and boundary management: the role of accounting, in *IRSPM*, ed. XIX IRSPM Conference, 2015. Shaping the Future: Transforming Public Management—Re-Invention or "Revolution"? 30 March–1 April, (Birmingham, 2015)

T. Brandsen, M. Honingh. Distinguishing different types of coproduction: a conceptual analysis based on the classical definitions. Public Adm. Rev. (2015 in press). doi:10.1111/puar.12465

J. Brudney, R.E. England, Toward a definition coproduction concept. Public Adm. Rev. **43**, 59–65 (1983)

S. Carr, *Personalisation: A Rough Guide*, 2nd edn. (Social Care Institute for Excellence, London, 2010)

S. Carr, D. Robbins, *The Implementation of Individual Budget Schemes in Adult Social Care* (Social Care Institute for Excellence, London, 2009)

Department of Health, *Our Health, Our Care, Our Say* (2006)

S. Duffy, The economics of self-directed support. J. Integr. Care **15**, 26–37 (2007). doi:10.1108/14769018200700012

K. Ellis, Personalisation, ambiguity and conflict: Matland's model of policy implementation and the "transformation" of adult social care in England. Policy Polit. **43**, 239–254 (2015). doi:10.1332/030557312X655828

I. Ferguson, Increasing user choice or privatizing risk? The antinomies of personalization. Br. J. Soc. Work **37**, 387–403 (2007). doi:10.1093/bjsw/bcm016

M. Fotaki, Are all consumers the same? Choice in health, social care and education in England and elsewhere. Public Money Manag. **29**, 87–94 (2009). doi:10.1080/09540960902767956

A. Gardner, *Personalisation in Social Service* (London, 2011)

C. Glendinning, Increasing choice and control for older and disabled people: a critical review of new developments in England. Soc. Policy Adm. **42**, 451–469 (2008). doi:10.1111/j.1467-9515.2008.00617.x

C. Glendinning et al. *Evaluation of the Individual Budgets Pilot Programme Final Report.* (York, 2008)

C. Hatton, J. Waters, *The Second POET Survey of Personal Budget Holders and Carers 2013* (Think Local Act Personal, London, 2013)

S. Hunter, P. Ritchie, *Co-production and Personalisation in Social Care: Changing Relationships in the Provision of Social Care* (2007)

I&DeA, *Transforming Adult Social Care: Access to Information, Advice and Advocacy* (London, 2009)

J. Junne, C. Huber, The risk of users' choice: exploring the case of direct payments in German social care. Health Risk Soc. **16**, 631–648 (2014). doi:10.1080/13698575.2014.973836

C. Leadbeater, *Personalisation Through Participation: A New Script for Public Services* (London, 2004)

M.H. Moore, *Creating Public Value: Strategic Management in Government* (Harvard University Press, Cambridge MA, 1995)

C. Needham, Personalization: from story-line to practice. Soc. Policy Adm. **45**, 54–68 (2011). doi:10.1111/j.1467-9515.2010.00753.x

C. Needham, Q. Mary, S. Carr, *Emerging Evidence Base for Adult Social Care Transformation* (SCIE Res, Brief, 2012). 31

S.P. Osborne, The new public governance? Public Manag. Rev. **8**, 377–387 (2006). doi:10.1080/14719030600853022

S.P. Osborne, K. Strokosch, It takes two to tango? understanding the co-production of public services by integrating the services management and public administration perspectives. Br. J. Manag. **24**, S31–S47 (2013). doi:10.1111/1467-8551.12010

V. Pestoff, Citizens and co-production of welfare services. Public Manag. Rev. **8**, 503–519 (2006). doi:10.1080/14719030601022882

V. Pestoff, Towards a paradigm of democratic participation: citizen participation and co-production of personal social services in Sweden. Ann. Public Coop. Econ. **80**, 197–224 (2009). doi:10.1111/j.1467-8292.2009.00384.x

V. Pestoff, Co-production and Third Sector Social Services in Europe, in *New Public Governance, the Third Sector and Co-production*, ed. by V. Pestoff, T. Brandsen, B. Verschuere (Routledge, New York, 2012)

V. Pestoff et al., Patterns of co-production in public services. 37–41 (2006)

A. Realpe, L.M. Wallace, What is co-production? London (2010). doi:10.2805/87863

Social Care Institute for Excellence, *Co-production in Social Care: What it is and How to do it* (2013)

M. Wilberforce et al., Implementing consumer choice in long-term care: the impact of individual budgets on social care providers in England. Soc. Policy Adm. (2011). doi:10.1111/j.1467-9515.2011.00788.x

G. Wilson, Co-production and self-care: new approached to managing community care services for older people. Soc. Policy Adm. **28**, 236–250 (1994)

Chapter 5
Co-production in Action: The Case of an Italian Residential Care Home

Gaia Bassani, Cristiana Cattaneo and Giovanna Galizzi

5.1 Introduction

Co-production is an increasing debate within public management. "It goes to the heart both of effective public service delivery and of the role of public services in achieving other societal ends—such as social inclusion or citizen engagement" (Osborne et al. 2012). The recent financial crisis puts emphasises on governments' needs to find new methods for managing public services (Kickert 2012). After the focus on New Public Management (NPM) and other waves of reforms and fashion approaches, co-production is one of the most powerful ways to reach a good performance of services (for citizens) at a lower cost. In fact, in this way the organisation or the public authorities could focus on detailed needs of citizens according to their priorities. At the same time citizens could be their-selves a resource for the design and the delivery of the service.

Literature confers different meanings to the co-production process, even if this process is perceived as something external to the delivery of a public service. Traditionally, the social and, above all, the health care settings consider clients as passive receivers of the care (Abma and Baur 2014). Furthermore, it appears that an over-professionalization of care is at work in these contexts. Recently, in the study of the health and social care domain, some authors, first of all Osborne and Strokosch (2013), suggest to focus on a *relational approach*. This approach consists in stimulating the empowerment of service users creating a positive social environment. As Alford (2009) argues, the intrinsic interaction in this case is viewed as an ongoing process where the relation is not "one-off", as in the transactional perspective. The majority of public sectors dealings are ongoing because there is a deep involvement of mutual personal knowledge, engagement and interactions among the actors. Similar to Alford (2009), Abma and Baur (2014) say

G. Bassani (✉) · C. Cattaneo · G. Galizzi
University of Bergamo, Bergamo, Italy
e-mail: gaia.bassani@unibg.it

© The Author(s) 2016
M. Fugini et al. (eds.), *Co-production in the Public Sector*,
PoliMI SpringerBriefs, DOI 10.1007/978-3-319-30558-5_5

59

that care-ethics starts from a relational view on human beings. Thus, the relational approach entails the need for connectedness and dialogue, both among users and between users and service staff.

Based on this approach, Osborne and Strokosch's (2013) propose a reconceptualisation of the nature of health and social services with the contribution of all the actors. Actors (e.g., physicians, nurses, managers, families, residents) could be engaged in the delivery or in the creation of the service, respectively. Actors could co-produce at the operational or the strategic level. Previously, this perspective was already adopted by some authors (Bovaird 2007; Carman et al. 2013; Scott and Baehler 2011), although they labelled these levels differently. For example, Bovaird (2007) argued that co-production activities could be viewed as logistic and governance drivers; or Carman et al. (2013) introduced the direct care perspective and organisational design-governance together with policy making as a more strategic perspective. Although the object of analysis is different, both these levels entailed the interaction and the active participation of actors.

Moreover, in the panorama of contributions referring to factors of co-production (Abma and Baur 2014; Alford 2014; Bovaird 2007; Bovaird and Loeffler 2012; Carman et al. 2013; Dunston et al. 2009; Gilardi et al. 2014; Sorrentino et al. 2015; Verschuere et al. 2012), some authors have proposed a range of motivations, facilitators, key variables and barriers to co-produce. There are just a few attempts to systematise these factors by associating each of them with the level of analysis (Gilardi et al. 2014; Verschuere et al. 2012).

Although the proposed studies take the relational approach and/or the peculiarities of the third sector into consideration, authors still have not clearly shown how this understanding of the co-production process works in practice. Thus, taking this broad perspective, the present contribution is the exploration of contingencies arising from the distinctions occurring when co-production is seen through various lenses. Specifically, adopting Osborne and Strokosch's (2013) point of view, the paper aims, firstly, at tracing out factors related to both the operational and strategic levels of analysis and, secondly, at identifying intertwined factors that enhance co-production at both levels.

The resulting framework of analysis has implications both for academics and for practitioners. Theoretically, it acts firstly as stimulus for enhancing innovative modalities of services and secondly as a map for integrating different literature and results. Empirically, the framework could drive managers and consultants to plan and execute co-production relationships, and policy makers to take the activities working at operational level into consideration.

Both scholars and practitioners could also benefit from a field exploration of factors in a 67-bed Italian residential care home involved in an important process of change. The methods applied to recognize the factors in the case study mostly follow the relational approach: one formal meeting, frequent informal meetings, the analysis of documents and familiarity of the context by one of the researchers. The period of data collection and analysis covers 2 years and a half.

The remainder of this chapter is organised as follows. Section 5.2 describes the levels and factors discussed in the co-production literature on health and social care domain. Section 5.3 provides a description of the case of the residential care home. Section 5.4 discusses findings and Sect. 5.5 presents the conclusion.

5.2   Co-production in the Social and Health Domain

The concept of 'co-production' is taking place more and more in public services, including new approaches to adult social and long-term care. As described in the Chap. 1 of the book, we refer to health and social care interpretations of co-production. In this domain, the concept of co-production is confused with that of patient engagement. In fact, as Barello et al. (2014) point out, it is difficult to define patient engagement because authors often use synonyms when describing their empirical analysis. One of the reasons for the poorly controlled proliferation of different concepts is that in services the distinction between production and consumption cannot always be separated. In fact, according to Fledderus et al. (2015) services cannot be produced in a standard way, the service results from the ongoing interaction between the user and the provider.

As the interaction is a social process, the distinction between consumption and production as far as time and place are concerned is beyond human control. Osborne and Strokosch (2013) refer to residential care homes as one of the most appropriate fields of study in which "direct face-to-face contact between the service user and the service provider" can be observed. In these settings, co-production activities appear guided by a relational framework (Abma and Baur 2014). Participation contributes towards creating a positive social environment in which care is perceived as a human need and an activity essential to well-being. Consumers, professionals are all involved together within the service development process (Dunston et al. 2009). Providers in this sense are not the only insiders of the process, as in the traditional health care approach. The professional knowledge required from the doctors, nurses and managers is continuously combined with the knowledge of the inherent in the patient him/herself. The context, thus, appears characterized by intense relationships and mutual support between actors of the health care process.

In this perspective, the distinction between the different phases of engagement introduced by various authors also appears confused. As Osborne and Strokosch (2013) suggest with their theoretical framework regarding *enhanced co-production*, there are, basically, two different levels of co-production. The operational level refers to the inseparability of consumption and production activities as pointed out before. The strategic level is more concerned with the intention to affect the strategic design of the service. In this way, the public service system could address users' needs more effectively in the future.

Thus, the enhanced co-production is based on a relational approach and entails both operational and strategic understanding. This perspective highlights the ideas offered by Bovaird (2007), Carman et al. (2013) and Scott and Baehler (2011). Bovaird (2007) adopts organisational motivations distinguishing logistical (or feasibility) drivers from governance drivers. Respectively, the first drivers arise when some services cannot effectively be delivered and the second drivers respond to declines in governance capacity at local or national settings. Carman et al. (2013) examine the patient engagement (patient engagement includes patients, families, their representatives, and health professionals) as a continuum from consultation to shared decision-making. Due to the involvement of the actors, the information flows among the service users, service providers and the system increase along the entire continuum. This continuum is guaranteed by the engagement, firstly, at the individual level, secondly, at the organisational design and governance level and, thirdly, at the policy-making level. At the individual level, namely in direct care, engagement implies an integration of patients' values, experiences and expectations with diagnosis and daily treatments. At the organisational design and governance level, patients' values, backgrounds and perspectives are combined with the design and governance of health and social care organisations. Finally, at the policy-making level, patients participate in the development and evaluation of health care policies and planning. Scott and Baehler (2011) mention the distinction between the responsive and operational levels of public policy. Osborne and Strokosch (2013) in their theorisation label the two levels introduced by Scott and Baehler (2011) as operational and strategic domains respectively.

Analysing studies that pay attention to factors of co-production (Abma and Baur 2014; Alford 2014; Bovaird 2007; Bovaird and Loeffler 2012; Carman et al. 2013; Dunston et al. 2009; Gilardi et al. 2014; Sorrentino et al. 2015; Verschuere et al 2012), some considerations may be outlined.

- First, studies use different names to identify factors that display co-production in action. These factors refer to actions, processes, structures (Carman et al. 2013) and intangible aspects. Moreover, they are usually categorized as motivations, facilitators, key variables and barriers.
- Secondly, the factors described by the various authors have an intrinsic balance between tangible and intangible elements. For example, in some cases, authors describe specific actions on the field, while in other cases they mention just trust, or values and skills.
- Thirdly, the health and social care domain, under the co-production umbrella, mostly involves in-depth operational level studies or theoretical contributions about governance processes and actions.
- Fourthly, some factors could work for co-production both at the operational and strategic level (i.e., intertwined factors). Moreover, these factors are responsible for enhancing a bilateral construction of co-production processes and activities at the operational and at the strategic level. Considering the relational approach, the interactions between users and providers create the ground for innovative services and decision-making processes. Thus, factors working at both levels increase co-production activities.

Some authors, such as Gilardi et al. (2014) and Verschuere et al. (2012) provide a sort of systematisation of these factors through both levels. In fact, Gilardi et al. (2014) mention how the collaborative treatment works and show how chronic patients participate with physicians in decisions about their disease. Moreover, the study introduces the organisational level, considering how chronic patients' desires could affect the re-organisation of the entire health care service. Other authors consider the identification of core elements that reveal co-production in action. Verschuere et al. (2012), for example, focus on discovering elements (i.e., key variables) that make co-production effective. They refer to conditions under which co-production takes place (Ostrom 1990) and they deepen the analysis by referring to intra-organisational conditions, such as work processes and types of involved organisations. With work processes, the authors refer to a radical innovation of the entire organisational processes. All the processes have to be strategy-oriented and the clients are the object of attention of each process and activity. The second condition they mentioned, refers to the debate concerning how types of organisations (i.e., third sector, public and for-profit organisations) facilitate co-produced activities. Due to the lack of comparative studies, the debate is still unsolved.

In the light of the above considerations, we show in Table 5.1 firstly, the factors that work at the operational[1] and at the strategic levels of analysis and, secondly, they identify intertwined factors that enhance co-production at both levels. We are aware that some factors could contain both operational and strategic aspects.

5.3 The Case of a Residential Care Home

Hereinafter the research process (Sect. 5.3.1), the research context (Sect. 5.3.2) and then the empirical results concerning the factors of co-production revealed by the case (Sect. 5.3.3) are described.

5.3.1 Research Process

The results of the majority of studies about co-production originate from either an in-depth theoretical analysis (Alford 2014; Barello et al. 2014; Bovaird and Loeffler 2012; Dunston et al. 2009; Fledderus et al. 2015; Osborne et al. 2012; Osborne and Strokosch 2013) or a fieldwork description (Bovaird 2007; Gilardi et al. 2014; Needham 2008; Sorrentino et al. 2015).

---

[1]As this study follows the distinction introduced by Osborne and Strokosch (2013), we aggregate both individual and collective factors at operational level. Consequently, we partially follow the categories introduced by previous studies (Gilardi et al. 2014; Sorrentino et al. 2015; Bracci and Chow 2016, Chap. 4 of this book).

Table 5.1 Factors at different levels of analysis

Factors at operational level	Patients' knowledge	Carman et al. (2013)
	Patients' attitudes and beliefs	Carman et al. (2013)
	Patients experience with the health care system	Gilardi et al. (2014)
	Patients self-efficacy	Carman et al. (2013)
	Patients functional capacity	Carman et al. (2013)
	Storytelling for well-being	Carman et al. (2013)
	Narration	Abma and Baur (2014)
	Creation of events	Abma and Baur (2014)
	Resident satisfaction	Abma and Baur (2014)
	Discovery of common ground	Abma and Baur (2014)
	Recognition and mutual understanding of underlying values	Abma and Baur (2014)
	All parties felt acknowledged for their ability to contribute	Abma and Baur (2014)
	Clients and professionals can be partners in creating practice improvements	Gilardi et al. (2014)
	Feeling of shared responsibility about the treatment	Abma and Baur (2014)
	Managing conflicts arising between patients and physicians	Abma and Baur (2014)
		Gilardi et al. (2014)
		Gilardi et al. (2014)
		Gilardi et al. (2014)
Factors at strategic level	Hospital policies that enable families to visit 24/day	Carman et al. (2013)
	Bedside rounding	Carman et al. (2013)
	Patient centered discharge planning	Carman et al. (2013)
	Electronic health records that patients can access and edit	Carman et al. (2013)
	Internal reorganization of the service	Gilardi et al. (2014)
	Create forums	Needham (2008)
	Allowing bureaucrats and citizens to explain their perspective and listen to others	Needham (2008)
	Need to find a balance between adding value for service users or clients and adding value for the community of the general citizenry	Verschuere et al. (2012)

(continued)

Table 5.1 (continued)

Intertwined factors working at both the levels	
Trust	Bovaird (2007)
Taking risk	Abma and Baur (2014)
Cultural change and resistance	Fledderus et al. (2015)
Learning and experience	Needham (2008)
Interaction	Verschuere et al. (2012)
Openness	Bovaird (2007)
Mutual respect for both expert and experiential knowledge	Bovaird and Loeffler (2012)
Identification of a facilitator	Dunston et al. (2009)
Fear of sanctions	Dunston et al. (2009)
Material self-interest	Bovaird (2012)
Intrinsic rewards	Needham (2008)
Sociality	Abma and Baur (2014)
Normative appeals	Abma and Baur (2014)
A sense of group affiliation and belonging	Abma and Baur (2014)
Users ability	Alford (2014)
Motivation	Alford (2014)
Certainty to make a difference	Alford (2014)
Generating evidence of value for people, professionals, funders and auditor	Alford (2014)
Developing the professional skills to mainstream co-production	Alford (2014)
Overcoming the political and professional reluctance to lose status and 'control'	Alford (2014)
Promoting an increasing power (and powers) of users and local communities	Alford (2014)
Developing capacity of users and local communities	Fledderus et al. (2015)
	Bovaird and Loeffler (2012)
	Fledderus et al. (2015)
	Fledderus et al. (2015)
	Bovaird and Loeffler (2012)
	Bovaird and Loeffler (2012)
	Bovaird and Loeffler (2012)
	Bovaird and Loeffler (2012)
	Bovaird and Loeffler (2012)

In view of the purpose of this paper, we chose to conduct the case study analysis through a qualitative inquiry method. The research was conducted in a small residential care home for the elderly (67 beds) in northern Italy. The majority of residents have physical disabilities but they do not have mental illness. As Osborne and Strokosch (2013) suggest, a residential care home is an appropriate example for exploring co-production activities through a relational approach. Furthermore, Burns et al. (2012) point out that the experiences of the elderly in care homes remain an under-researched area.

Concerning the methods of inquiry, the researchers based their analysis on documents, informal meetings, observations and interviews. Data were collected from December 2012 to May 2015. This process was facilitated by the fact that one researcher has a relative among the residents. In fact, she/he was able to collect data during informal conversations (i.e., meetings with his/her relative, the relatives of other residents, the service staff and local government citizens informed of the residential care home facts) and through observations.

Simultaneously, all the researchers collected documents about the setting and, in particular, about the organisational change under way, the strategic projects for the future of the residential structure and the new managers, and on the relationships between the residential care home and the local government. This process was driven by some information collected during a formal meeting with the President of the residential care home.

Since the collected storylines follow different points of view (i.e., users' view, providers' view and citizens' view), triangulation activities were extremely important throughout the entire process of inquiry. Triangulation has been generally considered a process of using multiple perceptions to clarify meaning, verifying the repeatability of an observation or interpretation (Denzin 1970). In fact, through triangulation of notes taken during informal meetings and of documents, we clarified the various meaning given to terms and concepts by identifying the different ways the process of change and activities are seen. Thus, the co-production characteristics of the health and social care service emerge from the case.

5.3.2   Research Context

The residential care home investigated is located in a municipality in northern Italy. The residential care home was founded thirty years ago and although it has been a private foundation since 2003, it pursues public goals and receives public funds from the local and regional government. The transformation into a private foundation is the result of a national and regional welfare reform in the third sector launched in 2003. Governance relationships with the local government are well established. The mayor of the municipality in which the residential care home is located nominates both the president and the board of directors. This fact guarantees that the residential care home is at the service of the local government citizens who pay lower fees than neighbouring local government citizens do. Furthermore, the mayor could, for example, pass an ordinance to admit a citizen to the residential care home at the local government's own expense. The residential care home cannot refuse this ordinance.

For three years, this context has undergone profound changes regarding the management of all the processes. In July 2012, the mayor nominated both the president and the board of directors. This fact stimulated an important organisational change of the residential care home. As a consequence of this change, the chief medical officer and the supervisor changed as well. For 25 years, all the services were provided by a cooperative that has its own nurses, social assistants, health workers and other service staff. The contract with this cooperative ended in January 2013. Subsequently, the new president and the new chief medical officer worked with this cooperative only for 6 months.

During that period, given the change in the legislation and the non-compliance of the structure in terms of quality-safety standards, the president and the chief medical officer intensified their relations with the service staff in order to have a better understanding of the existing organization. If, on the one hand, the change led to improvements in the conditions of the residents, on the other hand, at that time, the initiatives appeared "not to be in favour of the residents", but rather in favour of a general rationalization of operating costs.

After a few months, due to the rationing of leisure activities, the reduction of time that residents stayed out of bed and the change of the care treatments, the residents became unhappy. During that time, guests and families were obviously upset and the president and members of the board of directors understood that the changes had led to a deterioration in the quality of care. Thus, in January 2013, the chief medical officer resigned and the contract with the cooperative expired. Since February 2013, a new cooperative has taken over, while in May a new chief medical officer was appointed. He is a geriatrician and is currently working in the organisation.

The centrality of residents' needs has been the general philosophy of the cooperative since its origins. After the first years of activity, the cooperative focused on health and social care services gaining experience in the management of residential care homes. In 2013, the cooperative had 360 workers with a turnover of approx. 10 million euro. The staff provides a complete service for the residents (i.e., health and social services, catering, laundry services, etc.).

Although the cooperative intended to improve the service to the residents, in April 2013, the families complained about a deep sense of confusion. In fact, low levels of assistance and the new activities did not find the residents' nor the relatives' approval. Family members complained profusely for about a month and a general state of dissatisfaction was evident (both inside and outside the residential care home). Some relatives complained directly to the president especially in cases where health care was considered as insufficient. The president, therefore, decided to convene a meeting to explain the changes that were occurring and to introduce the cooperative. This episode put the patients at the centre of the delivery of care.

From February 2013 to date, the main organisational changes affecting the establishment of a process of co-production have been:

- The re-organization of processes and activities that directly or indirectly involves the patients;
- The introduction of a physiatrist to support two physiotherapists already present in the home;
- The employment of an additional doctor to increase health care coverage. During the leisure activities this doctor wears a white coat to give a greater sense of security to the patients;
- The opportunity to discuss the care process with the chief medical officer who receives family members half an hour a day, 3 days a week;
- The introduction of a nursing manager, who coordinates the professional staff of the structure, is the referent in case of health issues with physicians and who provides information on the patients' health to the staff at the change of shift. Furthermore, the nursing manager is the person to whom all internal departments refer and also acts as the interface with family members for every need and request;
- The inclusion of a psychologist for the patients as well as for family members;
- The opportunity for a primary care physician in the town to visit the home whenever she/he wants. The doctor is very well known and well-liked by the people;
- The increase in the hours of leisure activities (from 20 h to 30 h/week);
- The establishment of an intranet system to share patients' documents.

From a cost point of view, these improvements in the management of the services led to an increase in fees in January 2014 and September 2014. In addition, since June 2014, the residential agreement was modified to include a fee for new entrants to cover the laundry service. After that, the president formally reassured the family members that there would be no further increases in the residential fees.

5.3.3 Empirical Results Regarding Co-production

The origin of the co-production process was the meeting held in April 2013 by the president of the residential care home. In particular, the meeting was an opportunity for both residents and relatives to highlight their dissatisfaction about actions introduced and that the new management wanted to introduce. The president of the residential care home and the head manager of the cooperative explained the reasons for any activities that were contested, collecting suggestions about how the care service could be possibly improved. On that occasion, the president suggested that a permanent committee was set up for relatives in order to allow them to participate actively in the production and delivery of the service.

During the meeting, at the end of the various speeches, the president and the manager of the cooperative discussed many points with the families in detail. After this time, the relatives perceived a real openness on the part of both the president and the cooperative staff. The day after the meeting, the president set up a box for anonymous complaints, especially from relatives who did not want to express publicly their disapproval of certain initiatives. In general, the president is very aware of the relatives' points of view. Probably, the fact that he and one of members of the board of directors have a relative amongst the residents should not be overlooked.

The requests made by the relatives at the meeting were all taken into account. Thus, there was an increase in the time devoted to leisure activities (and to those initiatives, which are explained below as examples of co-production), changes were made in the lunch and dinner times, as well as in the scheduling of the patients' daily hygiene. Furthermore, the patients were once again allowed to access the living room after dinner and the proposal to set visiting hours for relatives was abolished. Family members can visit the residential home 24 h/day.

This first episode stimulated several activities, related in particular to treatment of patients and pain management, entertainment (through group activities), well-being and delivery of quality services. Concerning treatment and pain management, each patient has an Individualized Plan of Treatment (IPT), which is discussed in a meeting with his/her relatives every 6 months. This meeting is attended by the medical director, the psychologist, the physiotherapist, the leisure activity staff, the nurse, the patient's own nurses, the social assistants, the health workers and other service staff involved with the daily care, the patients and their relatives. In these meetings, relatives can request clarifications about the treatment, as well as provide suggestions to enhance patients' well-being. These circumstances also promote a greater dialogue between the professionals, discussing courses of treatment, as well as specific situations regarding each patient. Of course, the physicians are always available to meet the patients and their relatives to talk about any change in therapy.

Many other activities refer to leisure time, such as handcrafts for Easter, Christmas dinner, the narration of the patients' life on his/her birthday, the creation of vegetable gardens and the setting up of workgroups for ad hoc situations. These activities are coherent with well-established patterns of residents' well-being and health care, but each of them is characterized by a wider involvement of the patient in the design, planning and realization of the events. The design of the event is based on residents' experience, with an active role in the delivery of the service. Moreover, the majority of activities are organized with the involvement and participation of family members, as well as volunteers. Every day the volunteers deliver snacks to the patients and they help the staff to take patients to the living room on the ground floor.

During the Christmas period, for example, the patients are involved in the preparation of the Christmas dinner. Some patients provide their recipes to prepare the menu. Others are involved in handicrafts for the creation of the dishes (using a vegetable peeler), while others prepare various centrepieces for the table and decorations. Some volunteers and any family members available are involved in preparing the tables and decorations. A similar situation occurs during the monthly birthday party. The service staff chooses a couple of residents to tell their life story during the event. This moment requires quite a long preparation beforehand. During the days prior to the party, the service staff interact with the residents for the purpose of finding out about their lives, preparing what they will say at the party and how they will tell their story (i.e., with music, a movie, etc.). Moreover, since 2014, some patients have been involved in the process of preparing and attending to a vegetable garden near the residential care home. They choose themselves what kind of vegetables to plant, at which time, etc. Furthermore, the staff organises many leisure meetings with the involvement of volunteers and family members (i.e., a concert in the square of the town, bingo, harvest festivals, harvest-peeling and cleaning corn on the cob, cherry picking). Furthermore, in 2015, a psychologist and a staff assistant designed a patient team to participate in 10–12 meetings. This could be considered as an active way to share ideas between patients and service staff. Selected patients were asked to retrace their memories chronologically and present them with drawings or by cutting pictures from magazines. The psychologist did not interface family members, but the project allowed the professionals to build a more detailed patient profile about his/her habits, his/her experiences and the memories that affect the psychological condition positively and negatively.

Furthermore, the changes in the care delivery process has had an important impact on the participation of patients and their relatives in improving the quality of services. First of all, the new services and the wide availability of the service staff to co-produce the delivery of care with residents and relatives are described in the new service charter. Given the physical and mental conditions of the residents, the relatives played an essential and strategic role in this process of revision by expressing the residents' points of view, their desires and their expectations.

Therefore, thanks to the active role played by the relatives, the president and the manager of the cooperative compared the quality of service provided with the residents' needs. They planned an improved service delivery together with the relatives. In this way, as described above, a general increase in the quality of care has been achieved, in both the health and social care dimensions. More specifically, over the last two years there has been an increase in the number of minutes devoted per week to residents' care (from 600 to 901 min/week).

Moreover, through the relatives, the voice of the residents urged the board of directors of the residential care home to endorse the construction of a clinic for both residents and outpatients. In this way, residents have specialist care close to the residential care home and at lower costs. Furthermore, the fees of the residential care home remain unchanged thanks to the revenue from the outpatients.

The president is a key factor in this story. In fact, he is involved in a variety of internal and external initiatives that affect the service delivery inside, and promote a different way of considering the users' voices outside the residential care home. The president coordinates a round table with the other presidents of nearby residential care homes. During these meetings, the president describes the service delivery in his organisation and promotes a common understanding of the service management among the presidents of the other residential care homes around the table.

The president also participates in regional meetings where political groups represent a variety of territorial residential care homes. In this context, he promotes increased activity on the part of each political group to create circumstances in which residential care homes can show their experiences, discuss their problems about regional funds and norms and promote themselves as service innovators.

Finally, the president attended a specific master's course at university designed for residential care home managers. Academics organise this course combining frontal lectures with intensive empirical sessions in which each participant describes the processes and the activities run at their residential care homes. The president exploits these moments to reveal the users' points of view of service delivery. Moreover, he provides some examples of how the active involvement of patients and their relatives improves the quality of his residents' care.

5.4 The Framework Based on Factors of Co-production: The Links Between Theory and Practice

The case study could be interpreted through the relational approach described by Osborne and Strokosch (2013). According to the aim of the paper, at the operational and strategic levels, some factors may be identified that, empirically, imply the direct care and the organisational design and governance of the examined residential care. Figure 5.1 summarises these aspects.

Starting from the operational level, several activities in the case study refer to the residents' satisfaction (Abma and Baur 2014). Firstly, the co-produced treatment. As pointed out in previous studies (Carman et al. 2013), patients and their relatives are continuously involved with the service staff in the definition of diagnosis and in the search for the best treatment. In particular, residents and relatives have many informal possibilities to discuss their points of view about the care and health situation with the various residential figures. Doctors are available during their time at the residential care home in addition to meetings held three times a week. Furthermore, during the IPT meetings, the actors usually have an intense discussion about all the activities the residents are involved in. As Carman et al. (2013) argue, these circumstances increase the patients' knowledge about their own attitudes, their beliefs and previous experiences with the healthcare system. Moreover, as Abma and Baur (2014) emphasise, the recognition and the mutual understanding of underlying values are factors that promote co-produced activities at operational level. During the meetings with relatives, which in the case study is labelled as the first co-production episode, the process of establishment of a mutual understanding is evident.

Secondly, the quality of the health service regarding pain management (increasing the availability of doctors and service staff) and resident independence facilitation (availability of physiotherapists) increases. As the residents' perceptions of the quality of the health service were low, the new management introduced new services and practices through which patients and their relatives feel they share the responsibility for the treatment (Gilardi et al. 2014). In two cases, relatives reported that they decided on the physical treatments directly with one of the physiotherapists. In one case, a resident increased the frequency of gym activities thanks to the

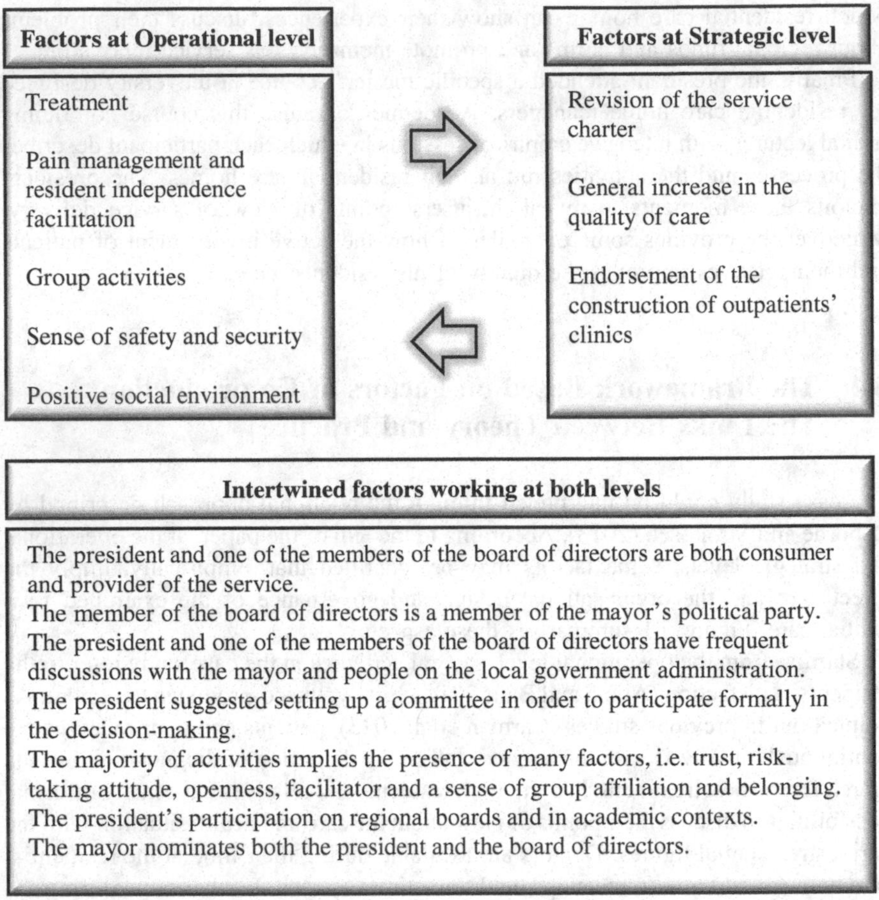

Factors at Operational level		Factors at Strategic level
Treatment	⇨	Revision of the service charter
Pain management and resident independence facilitation		General increase in the quality of care
Group activities		Endorsement of the construction of outpatients' clinics
Sense of safety and security	⇦	
Positive social environment		

Intertwined factors working at both levels

The president and one of the members of the board of directors are both consumer and provider of the service.
The member of the board of directors is a member of the mayor's political party.
The president and one of the members of the board of directors have frequent discussions with the mayor and people on the local government administration.
The president suggested setting up a committee in order to participate formally in the decision-making.
The majority of activities implies the presence of many factors, i.e. trust, risk-taking attitude, openness, facilitator and a sense of group affiliation and belonging.
The president's participation on regional boards and in academic contexts.
The mayor nominates both the president and the board of directors.

Fig. 5.1 Factors from the empirical evidence

collaboration of a physiotherapist and a relative. These new practices allow any party of the process to acknowledge the others (patients, families, doctors and all the residential home care staff) as a partner in creating a "well-being alliance" (Abma and Baur 2014; Gilardi et al. 2014).

Thirdly, the co-production activities allow access to a wide variety of group leisure activities. According to Abma and Baur (2014), storytelling, activities and events facilitate meaningful and appropriate social relationships, enforcing patients' attitudes (Carman et al. 2013; Gilardi et al. 2014), feelings and satisfaction among residents and their families (Abma and Baur 2014). Of particular importance is that the family is encouraged to maintain its involvement in the resident's life, given the emphasis placed on family contacts as a source of joy. Narration (Abma and Baur 2014) of the patients' life during the birthday parties is another factor that shows an intensive service co-production.

Fourthly, some activities increase a sense of safety and security, enhancing the patients' peace of mind. The opportunity to meet the doctors increases the residents' sense of serenity and well-being. Some residents mentioned it specifically, while others just smile more than before.

Finally, although the physical environment is important, a positive social environment is vital. As well as receiving good care from them, residents appear to need to develop a positive relationship with staff members, and to feel that the staff is available to them when needed.

Further, researchers identify both organisational and local policy-making factors working at strategic level. As Osborne and Strokosch (2013) point out, the strategic level shows the participation of users in the design and planning of the services.

The first factor works at the organisational level. As described in the case study, the residential care home policy and the reorganization of the services have been introduced in the service charter, putting the focus on co-production activities. The meetings with the relatives allowed both the president and the manager of the cooperative to change their point of view about the quality and the service delivery. In this way, the participation of the relatives drives the organisational change in the residential home (Gilardi et al. 2014).

Even the second element works at the organisational level, referring to the general increase of the quality of care in both health and well-being aspects. As described before, the first meeting between the president and the relatives was crucial for increasing a common understanding of the quality of residential care. Families clearly expressed the importance of increasing the amount of time per day in which the residential staff interact with each resident. The real increase in the care provided affects the entire delivery of the service and the residential care home policies (Carman et al. 2013). Regarding the change of organisational policies and the entire organisational process, Carman et al. (2013) describe other specific factors. Empirically, similar factors refer to the re-arrangement of the personnel management, the increase of space dedicated to health and care provision with the hiring of four physicians, the increased awareness of costs and managerial aspects (e.g., the introduction of a nurse manager and a controller) and the open door policy for relatives. As in Carman et al.'s (2013) field of study, the patients' electronic health records are available on the residential care home intranet.

Contrary to the previous factors described so far, others work at the local policy-making level. The local government contributes towards the payment of the increased costs by endorsing the construction of outpatient clinics for both residents and non-residents. The outpatient clinics opened in May 2015. Thanks to the income of the outpatient clinics, the mayor and the president will keep residential rates at the current level. During both the meetings, many families expressed the impossibility to pay additional rates. Keeping in mind these problems, the mayor favoured the construction of these additional care facilities adding this project to his mandate. Thus, the researchers identify this element as evidence of the change of policy at the local government level.

All these co-produced activities show intertwined factors that enhance co-production at operative and strategic level. Indeed, according to the relational approach offered by Carman et al. (2013), activities that increase engagement at the policy-making level may intensify engagement or improve outcomes at the levels of direct care or organizational design and governance and vice versa.

In the case study, the researchers identify the innovative process of change and the values forwarded by the cooperative as an intertwined factor (Dunston et al. 2009). Additionally, an important factor that links improvements at both levels is the fact that the president of the residential care home and one of the members of the board of directors are both consumer and provider of the service. Furthermore, a member of the board of directors belongs to the same political party as the mayor. Both the president and this member have frequent discussions with the mayor and people on the local government administration. Both these statements are similar to what Bovaird and Loeffler (2012) refer to as overcoming the political and professional reluctance to lose status and control.

Subsequently, another important factor could reflect Bovaird and Loeffler's (2012) suggestion to develop the capacity of users and local communities. The circumstance refers to when the president of the residential care home suggested to the residents' families to set up a committee. The families' committee has not been established yet because the relatives already feel they are engaged in the decision-making.

In general, all the meetings organized by the president could be interpreted as an attempt to develop a sense of co-produced service and of group affiliation and belonging (Alford 2014). Furthermore, the presence of trust (Bovaird 2007; Abma and Baur 2014; Fledderus et al. 2015; Needham 2008; Verschuere et al. 2012), risk-taking (Bovaird 2007; Bovaird and Loeffler 2012), openness (Abma and Baur 2014), facilitator (Abma and Baur 2014; Alford 2014) and a sense of group affiliation and belonging (Alford 2014) are intertwined factors observed in the majority of activities described.

The central role of the president and his presence on important boards are related to the process of generating evidence of value for people (Bovaird and Loeffler 2012). Finally, a less perceived factor empirically is that the mayor nominates both the president and the board of directors and this aspect guarantees an intrinsic coordination between the operational and strategic level.

5.5 Final Remarks and Agenda for Future Research

The adoption of a co-produced perspective in the health and social care domain strengthens the focus on process analysis. The peculiarity of this field of study is the intrinsic interaction among the actors involved in the delivery and creation of services. The authors describe this characteristic as the relational approach in which actors could co-produce at "operational" and "strategic" level. This is the first recommendation of the chapter.

Following the Osborne and Strokosch (2013) approach, the researchers offer a systematisation of factors working at both the operational and strategic levels.

Subsequently, they show how some factors work at both levels providing a clear link between the two levels. Researchers label these factors as intertwined factors. Although the authors map a few studies that associate factors with the level of analysis, none of them theorise intertwined factors. For this reason, this is the aim of the present study. The framework depicted in Table 5.1 is the second recommendation of the chapter.

As Osborne and Strokosch (2013) theoretically assume, the integration of co-production at both the operational and strategic levels transforms service delivery and co-creates new public services. This is the case of the services (for residents and citizens) provided by the outpatients' clinics. The multitude of co-production activities working at operational and strategic levels gives rise to the delivery of the most needed healthcare services. Thus, the third recommendation of the chapter refers to what Osborne and Strokosch (2013, p. S31) called the "potential for transformational change in public services".

Scholars could benefit from these theoretically and empirically based recommendations to nurture further ideas and investigations. Practitioners (i.e., public managers and consultants) could develop their understanding about co-production through the examples of factors working at operational and strategic level. In particular, the integration between service management and public management perspectives drives practitioners in the field to promote a co-production agenda. In political contexts where policy makers are not strong promoters of citizens' involvement, as in Italy, the framework provides the levers for the design and implementation of innovative co-produced public services.

References

T.A. Abma, V.E. Baur, User involvement in long-term care. Towards a relational care-ethics approach. Health Exp. **17**, 1–12 (2014). doi:10.1111/hex.12202

J. Alford, *Engaging Public Sector Clients: From Service-Delivery to Co-production* (Palgrave Macmillan, Basingstoke, 2009)

J. Alford, The multiple facets of co-production: Building on the work of Elinor Ostrom. Pub. Man. Rev. **16**, 299–316 (2014). doi:10.1080/14719037.2013.806578

S. Barello, G. Graffigna, M. Savarese, A.C. Bosio, Engaging patients in health management: Towards a preliminary theoretical conceptualization. Psi Sal. **3**, 11–33 (2014). doi:10.3280/PDS2014-003002

T. Bovaird, Beyond engagement and participation: User and community coproduction of public services. Pub. Man. Rev. 846–860 (2007). doi:10.1111/j.1540-6210.2007.00773.x

T. Bovaird, E. Löeffler, From engagement to co-production: The contribution of users and communities to outcomes and public value. Voluntas **23**, 1119–1138 (2012). doi:10.1007/s11266-012-9309-6

E. Bracci, D. Chow, When is personalisation considered a form of co-production? The case of Personal Budgets reform in *English social care*, eds. by E. Bracci, M.G. Fugini, M. Sicilia (Co-production in the Public Sector, Springer, 2016)

D. Burns, P. Hyde, A. Killett, F. Poland, R. Gray, Participatory organizational research: Examining voice in the co-production of knowledge. Br. J. Manag. **25**, 133–144 (2012). doi:10.1111/j.1467-8551.2012.00841.x

K.L. Carman, P. Dardess, M. Maurer, S. Sofaer, K. Adams, C. Bechtel, J. Sweeney, Patient and family engagement: A framework for understanding the elements and developing interventions and policies. Health Aff. **32**, 223–231 (2013). doi:10.1377/hlthaff.2012.1133

N.K. Denzin, *The Research Act in Sociology* (Aldine, Chicago, 1970)

R. Dunston, A. Lee, D. Boud, P. Brodie, M. Chiarella, Co-production and health system reform—From re-imaging to re-making. Aust. J Pub Adm. **68**, 39–52 (2009). doi:10.1111/j.1467-8500.2008.00608.x

J. Fledderus, T. Brandsen, M.E. Honingh, User co-production of public service delivery: An uncertainty approach. Pub. Policy Adm. **30**, 145–164 (2015). doi:10.1177/0952076715572362

S. Gilardi, C. Guglielmetti, S. Casati, P. Monti, Promuovere l'engagement dei pazienti con malattie croniche: Un percorso di ricerca collaborativa. Psi Sal. **3**, 58–79 (2014). doi:10.3280/PDS2014-003004

W. Kickert, State responses to the fiscal crisis in Britain, Germany and the Netherlands. Pub. Man. Rev. **14**, 299–309 (2012). doi:10.1080/14719037.2011.637410

C. Needham, Realising the potential of co-production: Negotiating improvements in public services. Soc. Policy Soc. **7**, 221–231 (2008). doi:10.1017/S1474746407004174

S.P. Osborne, K. Strokosch, It takes two to Tango? Understanding the co-production of public services by integrating the services management and public administration perspectives. Br. J. Manag. **24**, S31–S47 (2013). doi:10.1111/1467-8551.12010

S.P. Osborne, Z. Radnor, G. Nasi, A new theory for public service management? Toward a (public) service-dominant approach. Am. Rev. Pub. Adm. **43**, 135–158 (2012). doi:10.1177/0275074012466935

E. Ostrom, *Governing the Commons: The Evolution of Institutions for Collective Action* (Cambridge University Press, New York, 1990)

C. Scott, K. Baehler, *Adding Value to Policy Analysis and Advice* (UNSW Press, Sydney, 2011)

M. Sorrentino, C. Guglielmetti, S. Gilardi, M. Marsilio, Health care services and the co-production puzzle: Filling in the blanks. Adm. Soc. **9**, 1–26 (2015). doi:10.1177/0095399715593317

B. Verschuere, T. Brandsen, V. Pestoff, Co-production: The state of the art in research and the future agenda. Voluntas **23**,1083–1101 (2012). doi:10.1007/s11266-012-9307-8

Chapter 6
Co-production in Healthcare: Moving Patient Engagement Towards a Managerial Approach

Silvia Gilardi, Chiara Guglielmetti, Marta Marsilio
and Maddalena Sorrentino

6.1 Introduction

In the European debate on public policies, co-production is suggested as an innovative way to organise and manage services and to develop 'a smart, sustainable and inclusive Europe by 2020' (European Commission 2010).

The healthcare system is one of the most elective co-production domains in the public sector (Department of Health 2006; Voorberg et al. 2014). The application of co-production is believed decisive for the achievement of necessary healthcare service improvement and system sustainability (Dunston et al. 2009).

At present, healthcare managers at different organization levels must cope with increasing and changing demands, while resources to provide them are decreasing. The population is becoming older, with multi-faceted needs and high expectations, and the rates of chronic diseases are growing. This puts the onus on western healthcare systems to contain costs without detracting from the high quality of care. Rising hospitalization costs are pushing healthcare administrators to reduce the length of hospital stays and the readmission rate, making it necessary to build relational models in which the patient feels part of the healthcare team and willing and able to continue self-care after discharge. This is especially the case for chronically ill patients where the relationship is longer term and involves repeated interactions with and between the professional staff (Verschuere et al. 2012).

S. Gilardi
Department of Social and Political Sciences, Centro Icona (Centre for Organizational
Innovation in Public Administrations), University of Milan, Milano, Italy

C. Guglielmetti (✉) · M. Marsilio · M. Sorrentino
Department of Economics, Management and Quantitative Methods, Centro Icona (Centre for
Organizational Innovation in Public Administrations), University of Milan, Milano, Italy
e-mail: chiara.guglielmetti@unimi.it

M. Fugini et al. (eds.), Co-production in the Public Sector,
PoliMI SpringerBriefs, DOI 10.1007/978-3-319-30558-5_6

Berwick et al. (2008) identified a triple aim for health systems of the future: "improving the individual experience of care; improving the health of populations; and reducing the per capita costs of care". These three goals are interdependent and the challenge is to cultivate a balance among them. Co-production is spurring much interest as a solution to that puzzle. The US Center for Medicare services (McCannon and Berwick 2011), for example, identifies patient co-production as a crucial means to achieve a sustainable health system. A key factor of quality of the Innovative Care for Chronic Conditions (Bodenheimer et al. 2014) model now widely used to address the needs of patients with chronic conditions is the service's ability to encourage patients to play an active and responsible role in the management of their health.

Moreover, the evolution of individual behaviours as a result of the internet society has led to a growing awareness of new types of knowledge. In fact, the user-generated knowledge needed to develop more customized healthcare and social services through the effective participation of the people who use them (Realpe and Wallace 2010). The internet knowledge has challenged the assumption that physicians have sole control of the information (Coulter and Ellins 2006).

If the pressure towards co-produced health services is increasing, the debate is wide open on the nature of co-production, on how healthcare practices change in order to manage effective partnerships between clients and professionals and on the impacts of a co-produced service.

The healthcare literature makes a clear and convincing argument of the many and varied implications of co-production from the perspective of the individual (micro), i.e., the health professional-patient relationship. The in-depth and informed academic work has significantly improved our understanding of the implications on the clinical front. However, the impact of co-production implementation on the service management practices has failed to draw much attention in terms of either reflection or empirical knowledge. The overall contribution of the theoretical and empirical studies that use the lens of the service provider organizations is still underdeveloped. In fact, the actual definition of the concept of co-production is defying the effort to carry out evidence-based research on co-production processes. In turn, this influences its operationalization and confuses any understanding of which initiatives are to be interpreted as authentic co-production services and their outcomes (Oliver et al. 2008).

The chapter argues that the time is ripe for the research to explore "both individual and collective aspects of … changing role for citizens" (Pestoff 2012) *in conjunction* with the organizational production and service delivery setting. Drawing on a qualitative review of the relevant literature in healthcare management and occupational health psychology as well as the authors' personal experience, the chapter explores three main issues:

1. the dominant co-production models discussed in the current healthcare literature debate;
2. the main enabling conditions of co-production in healthcare organizations; and
3. the lessons learned from the healthcare co-production efforts already implemented.

To draw a clearer picture of these issues while also breaking out of the cognitive box mentioned above, the chapter is divided into three parts. Section 6.2 tracks the features of the two main perspectives on co-production in healthcare literature, reconstructing the different ways in which these approaches answer the issues of who the co-producing health authors are; what the domains of co-production are; and how to stimulate and support patients in their role of co-producer. Section 6.3 discusses the organizational enabling conditions under which the co-production options can be better understandable and sustainable from the managerial perspective, also aided by selected case studies. Lastly, Sect. 6.4 develops certain recommendations for the healthcare managers, useful for promoting and sustaining the development of such co-production practices.

6.2 Co-production Models in Healthcare

The co-production approach assumes that service users are not passive recipients of care and recognises that they can be co-authors with professionals in the successful delivery of a practice (Thomas 2013).

In the healthcare debate, the assumption that patients must be actively involved in all decisions concerning their health and treatments is not new. But what does it mean exactly when patients actively participate in the production of a service of value? What does it impose, involve and imply?

The biomedical literature shows how the effort to clarify what it means to build a healthcare system based on the hands-on contribution of the patients has led the academic debate to grow many conceptual roots. In fact, as demonstrated by Menichetti et al. (2014) in their bibliometric analysis of literature in the health field on the role of patients (review period: 2002–2013), an array of key words has been used to indicate the active role of patients, such as involvement, activation, participation, empowerment, engagement. These concepts while generating several streams of studies, however, *were rarely used together in literature*. The bibliometric analysis has demonstrated a time trend in the scientific use of these words where *the concept of patient engagement temporally overtakes other terms*.

Integrating the analysis conducted by Menichetti and colleagues shows that apart from a few isolated contributions in the 1990s (Edgren 1998) the health field has only recently started to open its patient engagement mind-set to an explicit reflection of the concept of co-production (e.g., Sabadosa and Batalden 2014; Cramm and Nieboer 2014; Batalden et al. 2015; Realpe et al. 2015).

A targeted analysis of the healthcare literature highlights two main perspectives with which the co-production concept has been used until now. The first refers to co-production as the contributions of patients to manage their own health and focuses on individual patient engagement and how to stimulate and support patients' engagement in co-production. The second refers to co-production as the contributions of patients to the planning and delivery of healthcare services and focuses on how the production processes change when value is co-produced.

The next section describes how these two perspectives provide different answers to who the co-producing health authors are; what the domains of co-production are; and how to stimulate and support patients in their role of co-producers.

6.2.1 Co-production as Patient Engagement

The first perspective places healthcare co-production in the patient engagement dimension. Following the Osborne and Strokosch (2013) suggestions, we can slot it into the *consumer co-production* category, due to its particular focus on the engagement of the individual patient at the stage of treatment with the aim of engaging them as willing participants.

As Coulter says, "The focus on patient engagement stems from a belief that the actions of health professionals constitute only part of the effort necessary to help people cope with the effects of illness or disability and restore them to the best possible state of health. An equally, if not more, important part is played by patients themselves, their families, and communities as *coproducers of health*" (Coulter 2012, emphasis added).

Generally speaking, patient engagement has been defined as an ongoing process where patients actively participate in managing healthcare (Coulter et al. 2008). The debate on the nature of the engagement and what 'to be engaged' signifies tends to spotlight one lead player: the patient, meant as the user of the health service. Engagement therefore is conceptualized as a way to live the relationship with one's own health and sickness. Graffigna et al. (2015) defined patient engagement as a "process-like and multidimensional experience, resulting from the conjoint cognitive (think), emotional (feel), and conative (act) enactment of individuals towards their health management".

The many contributions that have attempted to underline the nature of patient engagement have focused on exclusively one or another aspect of enactment, which we address here using the most cited works.

Singling out the cognitive aspects of the engagement, Hibbard et al. (2004) identified activation as a dimension of engagement and proposed an operational definition of what it means to be active by examining the skills and beliefs that differentiate the active and the non-active patients. The authors suggest that patients who are activated "*believe* to have important roles to play in self-managing care, collaborating with providers, and maintaining their health; they *know* how to manage their condition and maintain functioning and prevent health declines; and they have the *skills and behavioural repertoire* to manage their condition, collaborate with their health providers, maintain their health functioning, and access appropriate and high-quality care" (Hibbard et al. 2004). Therefore, the active patients are aware of their role and have enough self-confidence to believe in their ability to manage their health.

Focusing on the emotional dimension of engagement, Graffigna et al. (2015) underlines how the engagement enacted by people with chronic illnesses stems from an emotional elaboration of the disease diagnosis and of its psychosocial effect on their life. Interviews and focus groups with chronic patients (Barello and Graffigna 2014; Graffigna et al. 2015) informed that the engaged patients seem to have accepted their illness and feel that their life can continue to have sense beyond the disease; the sense of their life having continuity regardless of the disease drives the will to manage their health.

In a study of the behavioural aspects of engagement, Gruman et al. (2010) concluded that the operative definition of engagement is "actions individuals must take to obtain the greatest benefit from the healthcare services available to them". The authors evidenced the two ways in which the behaviour of an engaged patient differs from that of a disengaged patient. First, they consider the approach to managing his/her health conditions (for example, monitoring of certain health indicators, managing pain, stress and the emotional effects of the disease, assessing healthcare options, also taking into account their personal needs, desires and possibilities). Second, they analyse how he/she manages the relationship with the healthcare professionals. The active behaviours of the chronically ill patients in their interaction with the healthcare staff include:

- gathering, updating and understanding health information;
- asking for explanations into the benefits and costs of the various treatments; negotiating their own healthcare plan;
- recognizing signs of danger, transparent reporting of their symptoms; and
- giving the healthcare staff appropriate feedback on the effects of the therapy.

In short, the core dimensions of patient engagement regard their attitude towards health and towards the clinical treatment: the main idea is that the patients co-produce when they contribute to the choices related to their health conditions and the relative treatment, that is they share information (expressing their needs and preferences) and share deliberation.

From this behavioural perspective, the aim of the health policies to promote patient engagement is conceptualized as to encourage change in patient attitudes and thus facilitate more responsible behaviour in the individual and reduce healthcare costs for the community. Coulter suggests that the goal of health policies "is to support and strengthen patients' determinations of their healthcare needs and self-care efforts with a view to obtaining maximum value and improved health outcomes" (Coulter 2012). In terms of service delivery, the impact on organizational practices consists mainly in introducing self-management education programmes to strengthen the various dimensions of patient engagement and, therefore, in educating and informing, so as to build knowledge, skills and self-confidence, and to promote the appropriate behaviours to self-manage one's disease.

One example is the Chronic Disease Self-Management Programs (CDSMP), the stated goal of which is "*to enable participants to build self-confidence to take part in maintaining their health and managing their chronic health conditions*" (p. 17). The training revolves around five core abilities: problem-solving, decision-making, resource utilization, formation of a patient-professional partnership, taking action

(National Council on Aging 2015). The process to activate the patient casts the clinician as co-actor, whose role is conceptualized as a support to patient self-management. The clinicians should teach patients how to set healthy goals or to self-monitor their conditions (Hibbard and Cunningham 2008). This translates into the need for clinicians to change their consultation approach (*co-productive consultations*, Realpe et al. 2015). The focus on exclusively the clinical relationship between patients and clinicians is evident also in Hibbard's proposal that the healthcare services introduce at least four levels to measure the patient activation. The author suggests that the clinicians should use sliding scales to measure the patient activation in order to formulate personalized actions aimed at raising their level of engagement, starting with the patient's actual situation (Hibbard and Cunningham 2008). That work method could be useful for reducing healthcare costs. In fact, Hibbard et al. (2013) conducted a longitudinal study (six months) on 33,163 chronically ill patients enrolled in a private non-profit healthcare organization in Minnesota, demonstrating that the per-patient cost of treatment of low-activation level patients was 21 % higher compared with the more active patients on the index of disease risk and independently of socio-demographic variables (age, gender, income).

The self-management education programmes aimed prevalently at patient engagement (Brady et al. 2013) have generated a number of positive results, but also highlight some of the limitations of this perspective, above all those related to questions of equity and temporal continuity. Regarding equity, lower levels of activation have been registered among minority groups (Alegría et al. 2014) and people with lower educational and socio-economic status. The empirical evidence is mixed on the potential of the self-management education programmes to promote engagement and activation in the most gravely ill patients or persons of low socio-economic status or those less informed about healthcare (Alegría et al. 2014). Further, some studies have shown that such programmes promote solely short-term improvements (Wilson et al. 2006; Greenhalgh 2009). Other studies have demonstrated that patient engagement is neither an on/off status nor a linear growth process that stabilizes once it has reached its peak. Rather, it tends to oscillate (Gilardi et al. 2014).

In short, current healthcare research is dominated by this first co-production perspective, which above all focuses on the patients (and their families) and on the clinical relationship between patients and clinicians. However, although the research in this perspective helps highlight the individual dimensions that characterized an engaged patient, it has not yet turned its attention to the organizational and managerial implications of the co-production service.

6.2.2   Co-production as a Managerial Tool

The second perspective shifts its conceptual focus from the patients as managers of their own health to that of co-production in healthcare explicitly in relation to the service management literature (see for example Edgren 1998; Batalden et al. 2015). The 1990s saw the largest industrialized countries start to question the assumptions underpinning the practices inspired by the principles of New Public Management (NPM), the market approach that they themselves were the first to adopt and a mind-set that the public administrations clung to for at least 20 years. However, the spread of New Public Governance (or NPG) led to the realization that co-production was an alternative model of delivery of services (Needham and Carr 2009; Pollitt and Bouckaert 2011). In line with that shift, Bovaird and Loeffler (2012) defined co-production as "the public sector and citizens making better use *of each other's* assets, resources and contributions to achieve better outcomes or improved efficiency."

Looking through the lens of the NPG logic reveals that the novel element of the co-production health and care-based approaches is not only recognition of the engagement of the patients, but also that taking on board the patient as a new partner in the production process could influence the methods used to organize and manage healthcare. For example, Tholstrup (2013) described a co-production initiative implemented in a gastroenterology department in which chronically ill patients carried out the diagnostic monitoring tests themselves, sent the results to the medical team, then received a phone call from the healthcare staff to confirm the absence of negative signs, eliminating the need to undergo an annual check-up. This reorganization of the service process reduced the waiting lists, increased patient satisfaction and improved the level of appropriateness of the request.

The study shows how co-production in action cannot be understood by merely focusing on the active role of the patients in the healthcare decision-making process. When the patients (and their families) are urged to get involved in the healthcare co-production effort, they do not just express their preferences but rather become service delivery partners, willing and able to independently manage an activity that was previously done by the healthcare professionals (e.g., clinical treatment, medication, self-monitoring of symptoms). Some researchers, studying customer participation in the provision of services, have even defined consumers as "partial employees" of the service providers and have discussed ways of managing such consumers (Bitner et al. 1997). The change in the production process can influence organizational routines and healthcare managerial practices. Recent empirical contributions (Sorrentino et al. 2015; Neri and Bordogna 2015) showed how the lack of engagement by hospital top management and community services networks can negatively impact the effective implementation of the co-production processes designed by the operational unit delivering the service.

Therefore, in this perspective, to define a co-production process it is necessary to clarify who is part of the co-production co-actor network, how the roles and responsibilities change, and which tools to use to manage risk and to coordinate and allocate resources.

Clearly the unit of analysis of a co-produced service cannot be confined to the relationship between the patient and their assigned healthcare team. Rather, it must necessarily adopt a *systemic* perspective that encompasses the patients, their informal caregivers, the organization and the internal staff deputized to deliver the service, and the other support service providers that act in a network logic (see for example the model suggested by Batalden et al. 2015).

The networked character of co-production is the engagement of a variety of partners for programme delivery and even goals definition (Posner 2004).

This perspective casts far more light also on the patient-partnership ecosystem. The fact that the clinical environment has superseded the logic of mere involvement implies an intense use of the actor-partnership method. As highlighted by Loeffler et al. (2013), the patient co-producer performs several roles: co-designer, co-executer, and co-evaluator of outcomes. It is possible to identify five partnership categories in the co-production system sphere: treatment decisions; service planning; service execution; service evaluation and re-planning; evaluation of health policies.

In addition, the role of the partner in the decisions related to the organization and delivery of the healthcare service can be carried out by both an individual subject (patient or informal caregiver) and a collective subject (patient associations). Some organizations, in fact, have brought in members of patient associations to their hospital boards; others have involved patient associations in the redesign of certain practices (e.g., informed consent, see Casati et al. 2010).

The research is starting to wake up to the limitations of a co-production approach centred exclusively on the activation of the patients during their treatment and on the patient-professional clinical relationship. Going beyond this horizon perforce implies the need to identify and implement the organizational enabling conditions across all system levels.

The point here is that the project design and implementation of a co-produced system needs to be better informed about the organizational and managerial issues related to the governance of such a system. We have found little evidence in healthcare literature attesting to either the analysis of such factors or the identification of potential tools for the design and management of healthcare co-production practices. That is surprising given the far higher number of contributions that address these aspects in other disciplinary fields, for instance, public administration and service management. The next section integrates the healthcare literature with the managerial and public administration studies to analyse the key organizational and managerial hurdles and implications inherent in a healthcare services co-production model.

6.3 Organizational Enabling Conditions

Organizations in healthcare settings generally manage interdependencies by "establishing routines, which help to achieve coordination by specifying the tasks to be performed and the sequence in which to perform them (e.g., clinical pathways); information systems, which facilitate coordination by providing a uniform infrastructure of information to all those participating in a common work process;

meetings ...; and boundary spanners, staff members whose primary task is to inte-grate the work of other people" (Winberg et al. 2007).

The choice of which coordination mechanism to adopt depends on the degree of stability and repetitiveness of the respective situations. Pestoff (2012) identified three types of relationships between professional staff and service recipients in the service production process: interdependence, supplementary, and complementary. *Interdependence* occurs when an organization cannot produce a service without the inputs of the recipients. Healthcare examples range from clinical consultations to programmes of health management training. Patient information is essential to clinical consultations to reach a diagnosis and to define a sustainable treatment. Self-management education programmes would be pointless without patient cooperation. *Supplementary* is when the patient replaces the regular providers in certain core process activities. Such is the case of home therapy, where the patient takes over the actions that are usually carried out by the healthcare staff. *Complementary* is when the medical staff continue to carry out the core service activity while the patients or their informal caregivers carry out certain secondary activities. Examples are the mutual assistance groups managed by patients or family members, or the support experiences offered by patients who offer to act as mentors for other patients. The three types of relationships between the professional staff and the service recipients show clearly the crucial organizational role played by three specific enabling conditions: the ability and availability of the staff; the design of the delivery processes; and the ability to manage organizational complexity.

6.3.1 Getting the Medical Staff on Board

Health professionals have a crucial role in enacting and maintaining patient engagement, above all for patients with chronic diseases (Cramm and Nieboer 2014) or minority patients (Alegría et al. 2014). However, we cannot take for granted that the healthcare staff will take on that job.

One example can help us to reflect on this aspect. Leone et al. (2012) have analysed two departments of a hospital in the United States for patients suffering heart failure. The departmental staff had decided to introduce a co-production model to the care management process with a specific focus on the discharge phase. In fact, the biggest healthcare problem with these patients was that 25 % of them had to be re-admitted to hospital within 30 days. The goal was to reduce the readmissions due to the economic cost to the hospital and to the personal cost to the patient. The practice introduced with the aim of promoting the co-production consisted of some standardized teaching programmes designed by the nurses for the discharge phase. The research analysed if and how the nurses applied the principles of co-production to the discharge teaching. The results showed that the new discharge-teaching project had been configured as a standardized learning rela-tionship where the nurse primarily acted as a trainer and, at most, checked the learning progress of the patient. However, the results produced no evidence of behaviour aimed at engaging the patient to create a joint plan to manage their life and their health once they had returned home (diet, physical exercise, self-monitoring of symptoms, relationship with general practitioner). In fact, little attention had been paid to the specific needs, abilities, and the availability of the patient and their family network precisely because the practice was standardized. At the same time, the responses of the nurses interviewed showed clearly that they were completely unaware of the gap between the way they managed the training relationship and the stated goal of delivering a co-produced consultation. Indeed, while the nurses believed they were dedicating much time to sustaining the patient partnership, behaviours in this direction were relatively scarce.

This case study demonstrates how teaming the co-production logic with existing practices based solely on the introduction of teaching (discharge training) can lead to changes of little impact. The professionals would often like to involve the patients but have neither the skills nor the tools to put these intentions into practice (Parrado et al. 2013). Other observers note how transforming the way of managing the patient relationship touches on aspects of professional identity, interiorized during the professional training and shared with their own community of practice (Dunston et al. 2009).

An engagement model that involves the patient and their family members disrupts the traditional asymmetry of the traditional power of the healthcare culture, which identifies the professional as the expert armed with specialized knowledge and attributes them with full responsibility for decisions they believe evidence-based. Despite the formal statements, the tacit assumptions of such a system seem to place little value on giving autonomy to the patient in the consultation process. As some studies observe (Wilson 2001; Morris and O'Neill 2006), some professionals do not believe in their patients' ability to contribute to their healthcare or to make appropriate decisions. Others perceive the patient's growing decisional autonomy as a threat (Wilson et al. 2006) because it increases the risk to the safety of the patients in question and has legal repercussions on the professionals themselves.

In the face of such a system of beliefs, the healthcare professionals tend to frame the active empowering of the patient exclusively in terms of a more aware adherence to the prescriptions. However, that only means they end up medicalizing the practices of patient engagement to safeguard their power of control without, in fact, changing the service delivery process.

6.3.2   Designing the Co-production Process

Designing a co-productive setting must not only go beyond the bilateral professional staff/patients relationship, but also consider the patient's role of healthcare management in its entirety. Edgren (1998) described an example of a teamwork approach adopted by Diakonhjemmet hospital in Oslo. The author analysed the treatment path of myocardial infarction patients from the intensive unit to discharge.

The professional cardiology team consisted of a cardiologist, a primary infarction nurse, a physiotherapist and a dietician; in turn, these core team members were connected with other professionals (e.g., social workers and occupational therapists) to enable them to optimize the management of the rehabilitation process. As soon as the patients arrived at the intensive care unit they were explicitly invited "*to be an active partner in their rehabilitation*" (see the information leaflet cited by Edgren 1998).

The study shows that to achieve the goal of effective cooperation it was necessary to design and implement a new work process that called for new roles, new activities and new coordination tools from outside of the medical team and between the hospital and the local services. For example, the nurse's role was expanded to include an introductory meeting with the patient to understand his/her needs and thoughts and to build together a nursing plan which *co-ordinated different activities in time regarding information and education*. The nurse was responsible for assessing how well the patient had absorbed the information on which the self-management of their health was based after discharge and organized teaching sessions in the event they realized the patient (or their family) needed more help to understand and use the information. The physician and a hospital pharmacist educated the patients to take the responsibility for dosing their medication. The internal coordination method adopted by the professional team was to hold a weekly meeting to align their actions with each patient's progress. The doctor and the nurse met each day to update on the patient's state of health. The 'Heart School' was introduced to enable the patients to become autonomous by providing support through weekly teaching sessions that brought the entire team together with the patients. These teaching sessions centred on small groups of patients and their relatives and continued also post-discharge in the event of individual patient needs. A new figure, a nurse on the hospital payroll, was appointed to mediate between the healthcare facility and the relevant council offices *to smooth the transition from hospital to home*. The last piece in the puzzle was to arrange for the college hospital to involve patients in teaching activities.

In this case, the professional team and the patients complement their knowledge and resources in the value production process. Moving towards a co-production treatment model led to a redesign of the whole process. In particular, the hospital created a distinct nursing profile by taking the important step of investing in specific continuous training. Unlike the previous case, nurses had a formal role as coordinator of the heart team with clear tasks and responsibility for the whole clinical pathway inside and outside the hospital.

The case study suggests that the implementation of a co-production process requires the integration of different providers (Ewert and Evers 2014). Therefore, the health professionals have to: (a) choose which coordinating mechanisms work best between the actors involved; and (b) plan how to manage enlarged organizational boundaries and inter-organizational operations.

6.3.3   Managing Organizational Complexity

Another empirical case shows that a co-produced practice increases both the complexity and the uncertainty of the organizational setting (Sorrentino et al. 2015; Guglielmetti et al. 2012; Gilardi et al. 2014). The case study refers to a collaborative research to assess and redesign a co-produced clinical practice (Outpatient Parental Antibiotic Therapy—OPAT) for patients affected by Cystic Fibrosis. OPAT is considered a co-production practice because patients are asked to self-manage their antibiotic treatment at home and then to deliver parts of the care process. The expected outcome was twofold: on the patient side, an improvement in the quality of life; on that of the hospital, the possibility to reduce admission waiting lists. The bioethics centre of the hospital (the promoter of the research), the healthcare professionals, two academic researchers (the first and second authors of this chapter) and the patient-representatives of the local Expert Patient Association formed the research group.

In terms of service production processes, the results highlighted that OPAT increased the complexity of the delivery process. The nurse was given the additional task of managing the patient's teaching activities. The patient assessment needed to obtain home therapy required a greater effort of coordination between the different professional figures (doctors, nurses, social workers) to inform the physicians about the social conditions of the patient, their resources and the degree of self-management skills developed prior to authorizing the home therapy. A new help desk facility managed by a nurse was set up to provide support to home therapy patients in the event of emergencies or unexpected developments. Outreach procedures were set up with other hospital departments to enable faster access in case of need.

The results evidenced that the co-production initiative sparked a host of uncertainties for both the patients and the professional staff. The patients, while attracted to the idea of a less intrusive home therapy to reduce the disease's impact on their personal and professional activities, also had to contend with the fear of not being up to personally administering the home therapy. The doctors likewise perceived many uncertainties and risks: risk to the patient because at home they may not be equipped to deal with the (albeit rare) possibility of an adverse reaction. Another risk was that without the physicians monitoring the patient might decide to reduce the doses and/or the duration of the therapy.

The doctors and the patients were all clear that a more efficacious management of the risks was dependent on building alliances with the services partly responsible for the patient during their home therapy outside the hospital's direct jurisdiction (e.g., general practitioner, home nursing, and the chemist filling the drugs prescription). To this end, the team decided to lay the foundations for the local institutional protocol agreements by filing for formal approval of the OPAT-designed procedure and its acceptance into the hospital system. However, the request was turned down and this indifference on the part of the institution's management had negative repercussions on maintaining the continuity of care across the organization's boundaries in the outside world. This inertia led the professional staff to restrict the use of this co-productive practice, which then led to friction in some patient relationships.

The case highlights the importance of the institutional aspects of co-producing. The way in which hospital management responds to the enabling of organizational conditions that support the co-produced processes of healthcare delivery is a critical factor in the implementation of co-production practices. When the idea prevails that the managerial effort concerns solely the interpersonal process between patients and healthcare, co-production is deprived of the protective context that allows the actors to cope with the difficulties and the challenges posed by a co-produced service and runs greater risk of becoming a mere ritual. Crossing organisational boundaries and developing partnerships with other institutions can become very difficult when the institutional level turns its back on the need for consolidated engagement. The lack of awareness of the institutional and inter-organisational implications of co-production can frustrate the willingness of patients, physicians, nurses, psychologists, social workers etc. to co-create a system that goes beyond the binary logic of patient-centred or provider-centred system to promote a higher order integrating practice position (Dunston et al. 2009).

There is no question about the fact that the organizational culture can influence and shape the design of co-productive work processes. The case illustrated by Edgren (1998), for instance, refers to a hospital guided by a system of shared beliefs and values focused on a holistic view of the human being, reflected also in the tools and resources provided by the team to implement the co-production process and in its recruitment policy. Organizational cultures founded on bureaucratic values that target exclusively cost-savings are more likely to resist system-wide change. Indeed, in organizations that perceive co-production as a tactic for specifically cutting costs, the costs of some of the activities do not magically disappear but are actually transferred to the patient. In similar way, the management and design factors that make patient engagement sustainable are dismissed as irrelevant and remain in the dark in organizational cultures where the predominant assumption is that the patient is the only actor who needs to change. Hence, the patients and their relatives are left alone to manage parts of the service themselves. This attitude can seriously undermine the motivation that actually drives patient engagement (Cepiku and Giordano 2014).

6.4 Co-production Recommendations for Healthcare Managers

The debate on how to implement efficacious and sustainable co-production in healthcare has shed light on three interrelated key factors: the professional education system; healthcare system redesign; and service evaluation methodologies.

6.4.1 Investing in the Education of Professionals

A relevant condition for improving healthcare services through the co-production approach is to rethink the health professional training/education models, not just the health education of citizens and patients (Dunston et al. 2009; Batalden et al. 2015). As shown earlier, co-production implies a change in method that calls for a relational exchange between the patients, their relatives and the medical staff. The approach to co-production assumes that all parties act as partners in the delivery of the service. To enable that principle to be put into practice it is necessary to ensure the engagement of both the patients and the healthcare staff. Health professionals have a crucial role in enacting and maintaining patient engagement, above all for patients with chronic diseases (Cramm and Nieboer 2014) or minority patients (Alegría et al. 2014). Co-producing a healthcare service requires that healthcare staff is able, available, and willing to engage in a co-productive consultation. Health professionals are called on to fill new roles and acquire new skills: Boyle et al. (2006) suggest a shift from 'fixers' to 'catalyzers'. This transition requires an improvement of 'soft skills' (such as active listening; summarizing; silence; enquiring about patient's ideas, beliefs, concerns and expectations; problem-solving communication) (Realpe and Wallace 2010). Moreover, a co-production consultation requires ability, strength and conviction to build a dialogical relationship and to manage negotiations with many types of patients (including the less educated, or patients from different ethnic backgrounds). Hence, the clinicians must know how to adapt their participatory style of communication to the specific preference of each patient (Lee and Lin 2010), according to the degree to which a patient wants to be involved in their healthcare decisions.

Nevertheless, the willingness to change the method of patient interaction does not come solely from the providers' learning of new behaviours and skills, but also involves the professional cultures of the health providers (Dunston et al. 2009). Hence, the fact that co-producing requires the medical staff to assume a new professional identity cannot be reduced to a mere question of individual choice and voluntary decision but implies that the entire curriculum and practice of medical and nursing education needs to make a paradigmatic shift.

6.4.2 Redesigning the Healthcare Process

The co-production process calls for both the patient and the medical team to share responsibility for the planning, management and assessment of the options available to optimize the patient's health conditions. To make the partnership effective it is necessary to develop organizational structures, organizational processes and managerial practices that facilitate the relations of the co-actors. Creating a sustainable co-production system therefore means investing resources in organizational redesign and introducing new practices to manage co-production (Cepiku and Giordano 2014).

As suggested by Liberati et al. (2015), "Hospitals might need to redesign and implement new specific organizational devices to engage patients and families at least as privileged informants of the perceived quality of care and of the overall care services and, whenever possible, as active co-producers of their care services". This implies that management must break out of the mechanistic organizing box and rejig its assumption that the patient is just another cog to be added to those of the existing organizational machine. This mechanistic view of co-production sees the patient as just another activity to pile on the provider's workload with no attempt to redefine the work goals and method. Therefore, there is no meaningful transformation of the service production method and the patients risk being left alone to manage their part of the activity with potentially negative consequences on the safety and the efficacy of the medical therapy itself.

According to Kidd et al. (2015) "Co-production needs to be integrated into all aspects of the organizations": the healthcare team must be given the resources and skills to enable them to work with the patient and/or their associations to redesign the work processes that underpin and sustain the co-producing effort. The directional role is far more relevant to, for example, patients with chronic diseases who require the support and assistance of an entire *network* of healthcare services to ensure continuity of care. Building co-production processes that extend beyond the boundaries of the hospital is an indispensable enabling condition for these patients in order to motivate and sustain their engagement.

6.4.3   Implementing a Service Evaluation System

Considering co-production from an organizational perspective implies the adoption of a performance evaluation system. The extant healthcare co-production studies have used mainly clinical indicators of outcomes. Moreover, very little attention is paid to the evaluation of the impact on the healthcare providers or of the long-term effects of this option (Cepiku and Giordano 2014), despite the arguments for sustainable co-production (Dunston et al. 2009) and the ability of co-production to increase organizational efficiency (Edgren 1998). In fact, few examples are yet available on the adoption of systems to assess, for instance, the impacts on the organizational workings or on the use of resources, budgeting and the cost of the procedure (Duffy and Fitzsimmons 2006; Hibbard et al. 2013). These studies have produced mixed results. As indicated in Sect. 6.2.1, above, Hibbard et al. (2013) demonstrated that the per-patient cost of treatment of low-activation level patients was higher than that of the more active patients. Duffy and Fitzsimmons (2006) showed no difference in terms of the efficiency score of service in the co-producer patient and non-co-producer patient.

Regardless of the results, it is important to underline how co-production operationalization in these studies has been based solely on patient activation or patient engagement indicators. The fact that there is still no agreed set of criteria designed specifically for assessing co-production outcomes is a roadblock to developing assessment tools that go deeper than the general quality checklists about aspects of patient engagement (Staniszewska et al. 2007). That is due to the lack of consensus on the definition of co-production itself. Considering co-production as a managerial tool, a system of performance evaluation has to consider the indicators of process and not just the indicators of the results. Indeed, the two key conditions to achieve the expected results are: (i) implementation of the organizational mechanisms to support a successful co-production; and (ii) the reciprocal engagement of all the different partners of the co-produced system (patients; informal care-givers; healthcare professionals; manager inside hospital; other providers in the external environment). Currently, most of the studies focus on the patients with validated tools available to assess the degree and type of patient engagement. In the future, it will be necessary to have valid systems that enable the assessment of the engagement of all the co-authors of a service delivery process, the potential obstacles, and the resources deployed to increase the system's capacity to design and implement a co-produced service.

6.5 Conclusion

Co-production is gaining wider traction as a potential solution to the current and future challenges of public healthcare. The chapter shows how combining conceptual and empirical contributions from different disciplinary fields can help untangle the complex knots of incorporating co-production into the healthcare system. Changing a provider-centred into a co-produced system has significant cultural and practical implications. In particular, the chapter has presented the two key patient-partnership perspectives currently debated by the biomedical literature. The first focuses on the engagement of the patients in decisions related to their healthcare treatment. This micro or individual approach currently holds sway but is blind to the organizational implications, seeing only the interpersonal level of the patient-clinician relationship.

The second, explicitly connected to the service management literature, emphasizes that taking on board the patient, as a new partner in the production process requires the healthcare system to embrace change at different levels: the patient-clinician relationship, the organizational design, and the governance of the network of healthcare services.

Integrating the healthcare literature with managerial and public administration contributions has highlighted three factors that are high on the list of the organizational plan: the skills and availability of the staff to co-produce parts of the service with the patients; the methods of designing the delivery processes; and the ability of top management to handle organizational complexity. Therefore, to support the implementation of a system-wide endeavour, the hospital administrators need to invest in the specialized training of staff and in adopting evaluation tools to measure the outcomes of the service on the patient and on the organization.

There is still a great deal to do in terms of analysing the managerial aspects of co-production, which means that both the academic community and the practitioners need to give significant thought to this as yet undeveloped dimension going forward. Further, to make co-production practice a feasible and organizationally 'visible' option in healthcare settings it would be advisable to develop methodologies and tools specifically geared to multidimensional performance evaluation.

References

M. Alegría, N. Carson, M. Flores, X. Li, P. Shi, A.S. Lessios, P.E. Shrout, Activation, self-management, engagement, and retention in behavioral health care a randomized clinical trial of the DECIDE intervention. JAMA Psychiatry 71(5), 557–565 (2014)

S. Barello, G. Graffigna, Engaging patients to recover life projectuality: An Italian cross-disease framework. Qual. Life Res. 24(5), 1087–1096 (2014)

M. Batalden, P. Batalden, P. Margolis, M. Seid, G. Armstrong, L. Opipari-Arrigan, H. Hartung, Coproduction of healthcare service. BNJ Qual. Saf., 1–9 (2015)

D. M. Berwick, T. W. Nolan, J. Whittington, The triple aim: care, health, and cost. Health Aff. 27 (3), 759–769 (2008)

M.J. Bitner, W.T. Faranda, A.R. Hubbert, V.A. Zeithaml, Customer contributions and roles in service delivery. J. Serv. Ind. Manage. 8(3), 193–205 (1997)

T. Bodenheimer, E.H. Wagner, K. Grumbach, Improving primary care for patients. JAMA 288 (15), 1909–1914 (2014)

T. Bovaird, E. Loeffler, From engagement to co-production: The contribution of users and communities to outcomes and public value. Voluntas 23(4), 1119–1138 (2012). http://doi.org/10.1007/s11266-012-9309-6

D. Boyle, S. Clark, S. Burns, Hidden Work: Co-production by People Outside Paid Employment (Joseph Rowntree Foundation, York, 2006)

T.J. Brady, L. Murphy, B.J. O'Colmain, D. Beauchesne, B. Daniels, M. Greenberg, D. Chervin, A meta-analysis of health status, health behaviors, and healthcare utilization outcomes of the chronic disease self-management program. Prev. Chronic Dis. 10(1), 120112 (2013)

S. Casati, P. Monti, F. Bonino, From actors to authors: A first account about the involvement of patients in the informed consent governance of a major Italian translational research hospital. J. Ambul. Care Manage. 33(3), 231–240 (2010)

D. Cepiku, F. Giordano, Co-production in developing countries: Insights from the community health workers experience. Public Manage. Rev. 16(3), 317–340 (2014)

A. Coulter, Patient engagement—what works? J. Ambul. Care Manage. 35(2), 80–89 (2012)

A. Coulter, J. Ellins, Patient-Focused Interventions: A Review of The Evidence (Picker Institute Europe 2006)

A. Coulter, S. Parsons, J. Askham, Where are the patients in decision-making about their own care ? (2008) Available at: http://www.who.int/management/general/decisionmaking/WhereArePatientsinDecisionMaking.pdf

J.M. Cramm, A.P. Nieboer, A longitudinal study to identify the in fluence of quality of chronic care delivery on productive interactions between patients and (teams of) healthcare professionals within disease management programmes, BMJ Open, 1–8 (2014). http://doi.org/10.1136/bmjopen-2014-005914

Department of Health, Our Health, Our Care, Our Say: A New Direction for Community Services, vol. 6737 (The Stationery Office 2006)

J.A. Duffy, N.J. Fitzsimmons, Identifying and studying "best-performing" services. An application of DEA to long-term care. Benchmarking Int. J. **13**(3), 232–251 (2006)

R. Dunston, A. Lee, D. Boud, P. Brodie, M. Chiarella, Co-production and health system reform—From re-imagining to re-making. Aust. J. Public Adm. **68**(1), 39–52 (2009)

L. Edgren, Co-production—an approach to cardiac rehabilitation from a service management perspective. J. Nurs. Manag. **6**, 77–85 (1998)

European Commission, *Europe 2020: A Strategy for Smart* (Communication from the Commission, Sustainable and Inclusive Growth, 2010)

B. Ewert, A. Evers, An ambiguous concept: on the meanings of co-production for health care users and user organizations? Voluntas, 25(2), 425–442. (2014) http://doi.org/10.1007/s11266-012-9345-2

S. Gilardi, C. Guglielmetti, S. Casati, P. Monti, Promuovere l'engagement dei pazienti con malattie croniche: Un percorso di ricerca collaborativa. Psicol. Della Sal. **3**, 58–79 (2014)

G. Graffigna, S. Barello, A. Bonanomi, E. Lozza, Measuring patient engagement: development and psychometric properties of the patient health engagement (PHE) scale. Front. Psychol. **6**, 1–10 (2015)

T. Greenhalgh, Patient and public involvement in chronic illness: beyond the expert patient. BMJ Clin. Res. Ed. **338** (2009)

J. Gruman, M.H. Rovner, M.E. French, D. Jeffress, S. Sofaer, D. Shaller, D.J. Prager, From patient education to patient engagement: Implications for the field of patient education. Patient Educ Couns. **78**(3), 350–356 (2010). http://doi.org/10.1016/j.pec.2010.02.002

C. Guglielmetti, S. Gilardi, S. Casati, P. Monti, Divenire partner del team di cura: qualità del servizio e senso di appartenenza negli adulti con Beta Talassemia Major. Psicol. Della Sal. **1**, 87–109 (2012)

J.H. Hibbard, J. Greene, V. Overton, Patients with lower activation associated with higher costs; delivery systems should know their patients' "scores". Health Aff. **32**(2), 216–222 (2013)

J.H. Hibbard, J. Stockard, E.R. Mahoney, M. Tusler, Development of the patient activation measure (PAM): Conceptualizing and measuring activation in patients and consumers. Health Serv. Res. **39**(4 Pt 1), 1005–1026 (2004). http://doi.org/10.1111/j.1475-6773.2004.00269.x

J. Hibbard, P. Cunningham, How engaged are consumers in their health and health care, and why does it matter? Res. Brief **8**, 1–9 (2008)

S. Kidd, A. Kenny, C. McKinstry, Exploring the meaning of recovery-oriented care: An action-research study. Int. J. Ment. Health Nurs., **24**(1), 38–48 (2015). http://doi.org/10.1111/inm.12095

Y.Y. Lee, J.L. Lin, Do patient autonomy preferences matter? Linking patient-centered care to patient-physician relationships and health outcomes. Soc. Sci. Med. **71**(10), 1811–1818 (2010)

R.P. Leone, C.A. Walker, L. Cox Curry, E.J. Agee, Application of a marketing concept to patient-centered care: Co-producing health with heart failure patients. Online J Issues Nurs **17** (2), 1 (2012)

E.G. Liberati, M. Gorli, L. Moja, L. Galuppo, S. Ripamonti, G. Scaratti, Exploring the practice of patient centered care: The role of ethnography and reflexivity. Soc. Sci. Med. **133**, 45–52 (2015). http://doi.org/10.1016/j.socscimed.2015.03.050

E. Loeffler, G. Power, T. Bovaird, F. Hine-Hughes, *Co-production of Health and Wellbeing in Scotland* (Governance International, Edinburgh, 2013)

J. McCannon, D.M. Berwick, A new frontier in patient safety. JAMA, J. Am. Med. Assoc. **3**(21), 2221–2222 (2011)

J. Menichetti, C. Libreri, E. Lozza, G. Graffigna, Giving patients a starring role in their own care: A bibliometric analysis of the on-going literature debate. Health Exp. (4), 1–13 (2014)

P. Morris, F. O'Neill, Preparing for patient-centred practice: developing the patient voice in health professional learning, in *Paper Presented at: Professional Lifelong Learning: Beyond Reflective Practice Conference* (University of Leeds 2006)

National Council on Aging, *Chronic Disease Self-Management Program National Summary of National and State Translational Research Findings* (2015)

C. Needham, S. Carr, Co-production: an emerging evidence base for adult social care transformation. Policing **8**(11), 1–18 (2009)

S. Neri, L. Bordogna, New challenges for public services social dialogue: Integrating service user and workforce involvement in Italy. Unpublished Working Paper (2015)

S.R. Oliver, R.W. Rees, L. Clarke-Jones, R. Milne, A.R. Oakley, J. Gabbay, G. Gyte, A multidimensional conceptual framework for analysing public involvement in health services research. Health Exp. **11**(1), 72–84 (2008)

S. P. Osborne, K. Strokosch, It takes two to tango? understanding the Co-production of public services by integrating the services management and public administration perspectives. Brit. J. Manage. **24**(S1), S31–S47 (2013)

S. Parrado, G.G. Van Ryzin, T. Bovaird, Correlates of co-production: evidence from a five-nation survey of citizens. Int. Public Manage. J. **16**(1), 85–112 (2013)

V. Pestoff, Co-production and third sector social services in Europe: Some concepts and evidence. Voluntas **23**(4), 1102–1118 (2012)

C. Pollitt, G. Bouckaert, *Public Management Reform: A Comparative Analysis—New Public Management, Governance, and the Neo-Weberian State* (Oxford University Press, Oxford, 2011)

P.L. Posner, Accountability challenges of third party governance, in *Paper Presented at: 20th Anniversary Structure and Organization of Government Research Committee of the International Political Science Association*, Vancouver, Canada (2004)

B.A. Realpe, L.M. Wallace, What is co production (2010). Available at: http://personcentredcare. health.org.uk/sites/default/files/resources/what_is_co-production.pdf

A.X. Realpe, L.M. Wallace, A.E. Adams, J.M. Kidd, The development of a prototype measure of the co-production of health in routine consultations for people with long-term conditions. Patient Educ. Couns. (2015)

K.A. Sabadosa, P.B. Batalden, The interdependent roles of patients, families and professionals in cystic fibrosis: a system for the coproduction of healthcare and its improvement. BMJ Qual. Saf. **23**(Suppl 1), i90–i94 (2014)

M. Sorrentino, C. Guglielmetti, S. Gilardi, M. Marsilio, Health care services and the coproduction puzzle: Filling in the blanks. Adm. Soc. (2015). http://doi.org/10.1177/0095399715593317

S.Staniszewska, N. Jones, M. Newburn, S. Marshall User involvement in the development of a research bid: barriers, enablers and impacts1. Health Expectations **10**(2), 173–183 (2007)

J. Tholstrup, Empowering patients to need less care and do better in highland hospital, South Sweden, in *Co-production of Health and Wellbeing in Scotland*, ed. by E. Loeffler, G. Power, T. Bovaird, F. Hine-Hughes (Governance International, Edinburgh, 2013), pp. 90–99

J.C. Thomas, Citizen, Customer, Partner: Rethinking the Place of the Public in Public Management. Public Adm. Rev. **73**(6), 786–796 (2013)

B. Verschuere, T. Brandsen, V. Pestoff, Co-production: The state of the art in research and the future agenda. Voluntas **23**(4), 1083–1101 (2012)

W.H. Voorberg, V.J.J.M. Bekkers, L.G. Tummers, A systematic review of co-creation and co-production: Embarking on the social innovation journey. Public Manage. Rev. 1–25 (2014)

P.M. Wilson, A policy analysis of the expert patient in the United Kingdom: Self-care as an expression of pastoral power? Health Soc. Care Community, **9**(3), 134–142 (2001). http://doi.org/10.1046/j.1365-2524.2001.00289.x

P.M. Wilson, S. Kendall, F. Brooks, Nurses' responses to expert patients: The rhetoric and reality of self-management in long-term conditions: A grounded theory study. Int. J. Nurs. Stud. **43** (7), 803–818 (2006)

D.B. Winberg, R. Lusenhop, J.H. Gittel, C.M. Kautz, Coordination between formal providers and informal caregivers. Health Care Manage. Rev. **32**(2), 140–149 (2007)

Chapter 7
Co-production Makes Cities Smarter: Citizens' Participation in Smart City Initiatives

Walter Castelnovo

7.1 Introduction

Smart cities are an emerging trend worldwide. Making cities smarter seems to be mandatory to allow cities to cope with the challenges deriving from population growth and increasing urbanization. In a 2014 report, the consulting company Frost & Sullivan identifies smart cities as one of the 10 global megatrend that could shape the next decade. Not only the smart city mega trend will drive urban development for the next decade, but it will also create huge business opportunities with a market value of $1.565 USD trillion by 2020, according to the report.

People play a central role in smart cities. 'Smart people/smart citizens' is generally considered as one of the fundamental dimensions of smart cities besides smart and sustainable economy, smart mobility, smart environment, smart governance and smart living (Giffinger et al. 2007). However, although smart people is most often considered as one of the dimensions of smart cities among others, smart citizens represent a fundamental enabling condition for smart cities: there cannot be a smart city without smart citizens, whereas citizens can contribute to make cities smarter even without living in cities implementing smart city initiatives. Consider, as an example, initiatives aimed at making cities more environmentally sustainable, which represents a fundamental objective for smart cities. Every such initiative impacts, directly or indirectly, on the citizens' lifestyles and it is deemed to failure if citizens are not willing to modify their lifestyles accordingly. On the contrary, by voluntarily adopting appropriate behaviors citizens can contribute to make a city more environmentally sustainable (i.e., smarter) even if that city has not assumed any initiative that would qualify it as a smart city.

The most commonly cited definitions of smart city explicitly refer to citizens as the direct or indirect beneficiaries of the smart city initiatives. However, besides

W. Castelnovo (✉)
University of Insubria, Varese, Italy
e-mail: walter.castelnovo@uninsubria.it

© The Author(s) 2016
M. Fugini et al. (eds.), *Co-production in the Public Sector*,
PoliMI SpringerBriefs, DOI 10.1007/978-3-319-30558-5_7

this view of citizens as passive recipients of the services delivered to them by the smart city, there is a different view that postulates an active role of citizens in the achievement of the smart city objectives. Under this view, citizens not only benefit from the services delivered by the city but also participate (under different forms and with different modalities) to the development of the smart city. Despite how innovative it is, every smart city initiative is deemed to failure if citizens do not collaborate, at least by assuming 'smart behaviors' and 'smart lifestyles'. In smart city initiatives the collaboration between those who design and deliver services and those who use services (the citizens) is the essential condition to yield the desired results, which is one of the main characteristics of co-production of public services (Bovaird 2007; Alford 2009; Bovaird and Loeffler 2012). From this point of view, acting as co-producers is a way for citizens to participate in smart city initiatives by providing their 'smartness' to make smarter the cities they live in.

Co-production can be considered as an enhanced form of participation in which citizens are actively involved in the design and implementation of public policies, based on a redistribution of power between government and citizens. Citizen's participation is most commonly considered as related to the decision-making processes. When enough power is given back to them, citizens can act as co-producers by taking part in the (smart) city's decisional processes. However, citizens can exert important influences on policy also through their participation in the execution of public programs (Whitaker 1980; Sharp 1980). When citizens are given back the power to decide whether and how to take part in the implementation of public programs they can act as (informed) co-producers in the implementation of smart city initiatives.

In this chapter, the concept of co-production, considered as an enhanced form of participation, is assumed as the analytical lens through which to look at citizens' participation in smart city initiatives. More specifically, the chapter considers how citizens can exert an influence on the success or failure of smart city initiatives by providing the information necessary for their implementation. Hence, the focus of the chapter is on the role citizens can play as sensors/information providers (Goodchild 2007). Of course, this limits the scope of the chapter. However, although citizens can play many other roles in smart city initiatives, the role of sensors/information providers is the only role citizens can play that is specific (not to say exclusive) to smart cities.

The chapter is organized as follows. With reference to the relevant literature, Sect. 7.2 discusses the concept of smart city and the way citizens can contribute to the achievements of the smart city strategic objectives. Section 7.3 introduces the theoretical framework that will be referred to in the discussion of citizens' participation in smart city initiatives. In this section, the well-known Arnstein's ladder of citizens' participation is described and the concept of co-production is introduced as an enhanced form of participation. Section 7.4 shows how, without re-balancing the power relationships between governments and citizens, any participation exercise risks to be little more than rhetoric. Section 7.5 discusses the role of citizens as sensors/information providers. It also considers under what conditions citizens playing this role can act as co-producers in the implementation of smart city initiatives. More specifically, it is considered what the re-balancing of the power relationships could mean when citizens play the sensor/information provider role. Finally, Sect. 7.6 draws some conclusion and indicates possible future research directions.

7.2 Smart Cities and Smart Citizens

Despite the global trend toward smart cities, it is still quite difficult to find a unique shared definition of what smart cities are. Indeed, many different definitions of smart cities can be found in the continuously growing (both scientific and grey) literature on smart cities. The variety of the available definitions is confirmed also by the number of published papers that are explicitly devoted to, or include, extensive reviews and comparisons among different concepts of smart city (see, just as an example, Nam and Pardo 2011; Chourabi et al. 2012; Deakin 2013). In this section, with reference to the relevant literature, two core components of the concept of smart city will be discussed, namely *smart ICT* and *smart people*. The aim of the discussion is to identify the role that ICT and people can play to make cities smarter.

The different conceptualizations of smart city that have been suggested in the smart city literature share the basic idea of a city well performing in all the sub-systems it comprises thanks to the intensive use of the Information and Communication Technologies (ICT) and with the aim of offering the best possible quality of life (more livable cities), with the lowest possible use of resources (more sustainable cities). Dirks and Keeling (2009) identify city services, citizens, business, transport, communication, water and energy as the sub-systems central to cities operation and development. This makes a smart city a system of interrelated sub-systems in which 'smartness' strictly depends on the organic integration of the sub-systems. Harrison and Donnelly (2011) explain the sub-systems integration in terms of interconnection and instrumentation that can be achieved by means of ICT. From this point of view, ICT can be considered as the basic infrastructure for smart cities.

The central role of ICT for the cities' smartness is extensively shared within the smart city literature. With the aim of proposing a standard and comprehensive definition of smart city, the International Telecommunication Union (ITU) analyzed 98 definitions of smart cities in the relevant literature (both scientific and grey) and found 49 key concepts/keywords that occur 573 times in the definitions considered. The ITU's survey shows that the key concepts/keywords most often used are those related to ICT that cover the 26 % of the occurrences of the 49 key concepts/keywords identified (ITU 2014). This led ITU to suggest a definition of smart city as a city that leverages the ICT infrastructure to improve citizens' quality of life and well-being, ensure sustainable economic growth, streamline city services, reinforce prevention of disasters and provide effective governance mechanisms. Under this conceptualization, that subsumes some of the most common definitions of smart city, smart cities aim at achieving an economically sustainable urban environment without sacrificing comfort, convenience and quality of life of citizenry. This objective can be achieved by using ICT as the 'great equalizer' (human to human, human to machine and machine to machine) to connect a variety of everyday living services to public infrastructures (ITU 2014).

As Chourabi et al. (2012) point out, smart city initiatives resemble e-government initiatives under many respects. This makes it possible to apply to smart city initiatives some lessons learned from past experiences in the implementation of e-government. Smart city initiatives seem to be characterized by the same government push approach that has been dominant in the e-government arena during the past decades (Reddick 2005; Kunstelj and Vintar 2004; Verdegem and Verleye 2009; Gauld et al. 2010). In the case of e-government, the government push approach led governments to expand the portfolio of the services delivered to citizens by creating online services most often driven by the technological possibilities rather than by the user needs (Verdegem and Verleye 2009). Similarly, most smart city initiatives have been, and are still being, characterized by vendor push (Belissent 2010; Schaffers et al. 2011) and by a technological driven vision that leads policy makers to (sometimes blindly) rely on the ability of technological solutions to manage urban spaces, administrative processes, knowledge and information (Galdon-Clavell 2013). The extensive use of ICT in smart city initiatives allows the development of ICT-enabled services for health, security and safety, governance, as well as the delivery of (new) public services. However, these services are most often (if not almost always) based on commercial technological solutions pushed by vendors (Hernandez-Munoz et al. 2011) and this impacts critically on the ability of the policy-makers to develop a strategic and coherent understanding of how smart technologies and smart environments could lead to better cities (Galdon-Clavell 2013).

The main problem with the government/vendor push approach in the smart city initiatives is that they fail to acknowledge that smart city solutions must start with the city not the smart (Belissent 2010; Schaffers et al. 2011). Starting from the city instead of starting from the 'smart' means, first of all, making smart solutions truly citizen-centric (Nam and Pardo 2011), which also means putting people at the core of smart cities instead of technologies.

Vanolo (2014) observes that smart city initiatives inevitably also co-produce smart people, if only because people have to be willing to adapt to, and to live in, smart cities. Hence, the way in which smart cities are conceptualized also determines how the concept of smart people is (implicitly or explicitly) characterized.

Virtually, all the most cited smart city frameworks explicitly refer to people as one of the systems a city comprises. According to Dirks and Keeling (2009), a smart city is one that invests in education, health, housing, public safety and social services and uses ICT and smart technologies for human and social services, with the aim of achieving higher levels of education, health, housing, public safety and social outcomes. According to Neirotti et al. (2014), to make citizens smarter a smart city has to implement measures to foster entrepreneurship, to improve human capital investment, to promote the use of ICT-based learning tools in schools and to manage and promote the city's cultural heritage. Lombardi et al. (2011) suggest measuring people's smartness by means of indicators such as the education level of citizens; the foreign language, computer and internet skills; the participation in life-long learning; the percentage of people working in education and in knowledge-intensive sectors; the patent applications per inhabitant; the voter turnout in elections and the share of female city representatives. Similarly, for Giffinger et al. (2007), people's smartness can be assessed by considering the level of qualification; the affinity to life-long learning; the social and ethnic plurality; the people's flexibility, creativity, cosmopolitanism/open-mindedness and the participation in public life. Chourabi et al. (2012) summarize the way people and communities are typically addressed as part of smart cities by observing that smart city initiatives are designed to have impacts on the quality of life of citizens and to foster more informed and educated citizens in order to allow them to participate in the governance and management of the city, thus becoming active users.

Although the government/vendor push approach dominant in the traditional smart city discourse tends to restrict a lot the role (smart) people can play, Chourabi et al. (2012) claim that citizens are key players that have the opportunity to engage with smart city initiatives to the extent that they can influence the effort to be a success or a failure. However, how can citizens influence the success or failure of smart city initiatives?

Besides as a possible source of complexity for cities, due to problems related to urbanization that makes the management of (larger and larger) cities critical (Harrison and Donnelly 2011; Dirks and Keeling 2009), in the smart city discourse people are mostly referred to: (i) as possible beneficiaries of the infrastructures and services smart cities can deliver (Cosgrave et al. 2014), and (ii) as active users that participate in the construction of smart cities and that are implicitly considered responsible for this objective (Brand 2007; Vanolo 2014).

By considering citizens as the users/beneficiaries of the city's smart infrastructures and services, the first and most obvious way in which citizens can influence the success or failure of a smart city initiative is determined by their willingness and capacity to adopt and use those infrastructures and services. In this case, in the conceptualization of smart citizens as 'active users' it is the 'user' part of the definition to be stressed. As Hollands (2015) points out, under this conceptualization, 'smart' is limited to being able to access, consume and use the new technology; citizens' smartness is thus reduced to a form of 'smart mentality', simply adopting the right frame of mind to accept and cope with the inevitability of urban technological change (p. 73).

This way of conceiving the success or failure of smart city initiatives strictly reminds the long lasting discussion on e-government success/failure factors (Carter and Bélanger 2005; Gil-García and Pardo 2005) from which some lessons can be learned that can be useful also in the context of smart cities. One of the main results that emerged from the discussion on e-government success/failure factors is that the users' adoption and use of innovative services strictly depends, among other things, on the perceived usefulness and the perceived ease of use of the services (Carter and Bélanger 2005). As reminded by Gauld et al. (2010), even projects that are successful in terms of technological and project development may face a failure if citizens simply do not use the systems implemented.

Despite what the decision makers and the service designers think it is useful for citizens, as highlighted by Gourville (2004), there is a mismatch of 9 to 1 between what innovators think consumers want and what consumers actually want. Thus, in most cases, citizens do not use innovative services either because they are not what they need more or because they do not see them as able to deliver a value and to improve the quality of their lives. As Olphert and Damodaran (2007) point out, to satisfy the critical success factors a good knowledge and understanding of the needs of prospective users is needed. Direct engagement with relevant individuals or groups in society is the richest, most revealing and valid source of knowledge about them (p. 501). This points to the need of overcoming both technological determinism and the supply-driven, top-down approach that tends to reduce citizens to active users of the services delivered, where 'active' simply means collaborative with respect to initiatives that are decided elsewhere and pushed by governments.

Contrary to the dominant supply-driven approach, and to avoid some of the problems that affected the success of many e-government projects, smart city initiatives should assume a demand-side approach instead. Indeed, as Nam and Pardo (2011) observe, policies in successful smart cities are demand-driven rather than supply-driven, or well-balanced between the two approaches. By assuming a demand-driven, bottom-up approach the focus is on people and their needs, priorities and expectations, shifting from governmental push for smart city initiatives to a non-governmental parties' engagement in them. This would make smart city initiatives more likely to meet the real needs of citizens, thus reducing the possible negative effects of the '9× problem' described by Gourville. In the conceptualization of smart citizens as 'active users' the demand-side approach highlights the 'active' part of the definition, shifting the focus from the citizens' use of infrastructures and services to citizens' engagement and participation. Citizens' engagement is both an enabling condition and a possible outcome of demand-driven policies in smart cities. Indeed, a smart city needs to create a community where all citizens can engage more easily and effectively, thus developing citizens' sense of ownership of their city, enhance the local authority's awareness of their needs, and ultimately reshape the citizen-government relationship (Nam and Pardo 2011).

Participation, like people, is one of the concepts most often referred to in the smart city literature. However, to make sense of the concept of participation, in general and in the context of smart cities in particular, it is necessary, first of all, to clearly distinguish participation from participatory approach. Indeed, participation does not necessarily entail the use of the tools and methodologies for enabling engagement and expression of voice typical of 'participatory' approaches (Standing 2004). Moreover, when talking about participation it is necessary to clarify, at least, what type of participation is referred to, who is participating, in what and for whose benefit (Cornwall 2008). Although citizens' participation is commonly viewed as attempts to influence the formulation of public policies, citizens exert important influences on policy also through their participation in the execution of public programs (Whitaker 1980; Sharp 1980). As observed by Whitaker (1980), this is particularly the case in human services where change in the clients' behavior is the 'product' that is supposed to be delivered (p. 240). This type of citizens' participation is the one relevant for the aims of the discussion in this chapter in which it will be considered how citizens can exert an influence on the success or failure of smart city initiatives through their participation in the execution of public programs as sensors/information providers.

7.3 Theoretical Frame: Citizens' Participation and Co-production

Participation is a central concept in the public policy discourse and, more generally, in the contemporary culture to the point that it has become one of the mantras of the digital age. However, as Cornwall (2008) points out, this widespread adoption of the language of participation raises questions about what exactly this much-used buzzword has come to mean, since 'participation' can be used to evoke almost anything that involves people.

The literature on citizens' participation is continuously growing, as it is the number of mechanisms and tools for supporting participation developed by scholars and practitioners. A review of the different typologies and models for citizens' participation suggested in the literature is out of the scope of this chapter (a quite comprehensive list of participation mechanisms is summarized in (Rowe and Frewer 2005)). For the present purposes, we can limit our attention to one of the most cited of them, namely the so-called Arnstein's ladder of citizens' participation (Arnstein 1969).

Although Arnstein's classification may appear obsolete and has been criticized as defective in some ways (Tritter and McCallum 2006; Fung 2006; Cornwall 2008), it will be used in the discussion of citizen's participation in smart city initiatives mainly for two reasons. First, (Arnstein 1969) is one the most cited works on citizens' participation in the academic and grey literature. Second, and more importantly, Arnstein's classification considers participation as valuable only to the extent that it involves a redistribution of power without which participation is 'an empty and frustrating process for the powerless. It allows the powerholders to claim that all sides were considered, but makes it possible for only some of those sides to benefit' (Arnstein 1969). By considering how power is possibly redistributed in the various levels of participation, Arnstein's classification helps to unveil the somewhat empty rhetoric that quite often characterizes discourses about citizens' participation. This makes Arnstein's classification a good starting point also for discussing citizens' participation in the context of smart cities in order to consider how and to what extent smart citizens can effectively exert an influence on the implementation of smart city initiatives. In doing so, the rungs of the ladder will not be considered as increasing levels leading to better and better forms of participation, which is one of the major criticisms to Arnstein's model (Tritter and McCallum 2006). Rather, the rungs of the Arnstein's ladder will be considered as the description of different 'participation configurations', either pushed by government initiatives or deriving from bottom-up citizens' initiatives, that can be more or less effective in particular contexts, in relation to different issues and at different times.

The Arnstein's ladder comprises eight rungs that can be grouped in three stages: Non-participation, Tokenism and Citizen Power. The participation modalities corresponding to the power distribution typical of the lowest rungs of the ladder do not enable people to participate, rather they enable power-holders to 'educate' (Manipulation) or 'cure' the participants (Therapy). The participation modalities typical of the stage of Tokenism allow the have-nots (citizens) to hear (Informing), have a voice (Consultation) and advise, although the power-holders retain the right to decide (Placation). Finally, in the stage of Citizen Power, citizens can engage in trade-offs with power-holders (Partnership), obtain the dominant decision-making authority in a plan or program (Delegated Power), or full managerial power (Citizen Control).

Partnership represents the first configuration of the power relationships in which citizens can exert a direct influence on policy making and, even more interesting for the aims of the present discussion, on the implementation of public programs. Starting from partnership, it makes sense to conceptualize citizens' participation as co-production, since in partnership citizens are required to provide some of the resources relevant for the implementation of public programs and services, based on an equal and reciprocal relationship between them and professionals, which according to Bovaird (2007) is what co-production amounts to.

As the extensive discussion of the concept in Chap. 1 shows, co-production is a value-creating activity that challenges the traditional conception of the value creation process with respect to the role of the users/consumers. Co-production is much more than user/consumer involvement. Prahalad and Ramaswamy (2004) observe that, in the more common variations of consumer involvement, the firm is still in charge of the overall orchestration of the experience, with consumers treated as passive. Managers partition some of the work usually done by the firm and pass it on to their consumers. The firm decides what products and services to produce and, by implication, it decides what counts as value and what is of value to the customers. Hence, consumers have little or no role in the value creation process. Co-production gives the users an active role in the (co)creation of value instead: it entails the redefinition of both the meaning of value and the process of value creation.

Bovaird and Löffler (2012) observe that there is a huge latent willingness of citizens to become more involved and to act as public services co-producers, but only if they feel that a value for people is created through co-production. Co-production always entails an effort on the part of the co-producers; to decide whether the effort was worthwhile, they need to compare the effectiveness of the co-production strategy in terms of a cost–benefit calculation (Etgar 2008). Purely selfish motivation on the part of users cannot explain completely their willingness to co-produce; people's motivation to co-produce depends on a wider array of factors than the individual self-interest of utility theory (Alford 2009). Users may also want to play an active role in service co-production to increase other elements of value-added, for instance environmental sustainability, social inclusion or the spreading of benefits across the widest possible range of local community members (Bovaird and Loeffler 2012). Hence, the value a citizen receives back as a compensation for the effort to co-produce is not only a value for him, but also possibly a value for the wider population and for future generations of citizens as well, i.e. a public value (Hartley 2011). Public value is the fundamental value created through the citizens' involvement as co-producers in the value creation process, which does not exclude that co-producers could get also a private value from their participation (Alford 2009; Bovaird and Loeffler 2012).

Smart city initiatives (at least programmatically) aim at generating benefits typically related to the 'public sphere'. Smart cities livability and sustainability involve values that extend beyond market economic considerations and include social, political, cultural and environmental dimensions (Benington 2011). The assessment of the results of smart city initiatives, based on a citizen centered approach and assuming a public value perspective (Cosgrave et al. 2014; Baccarne et al. 2014), provides the basis citizens can rely on to decide whether their effort to co-produce in smart city initiatives was worthwhile.

Citizens' involvement as co-producers in public value creation processes is the principle against which different examples of citizens' participation in smart city initiatives will be compared in the next two sections.

7.4 Participation Without Power Sharing

This section discusses some examples of citizens' participation in smart city initiatives to show how in many cases the use of the term 'participation' can be misleading and what re-balancing the power relationship between government and citizens could mean.

'Sustainable' is one of the most used qualification referred to smart cities. In the ITU (2014) survey, those related to environment and sustainability cover 16 % of the occurrences of key concepts/keywords in the most cited definitions of smart city. The idea of sustainable cities is built around problems concerning the availability of resources, energy flows, production and consumption patterns, waste and pollution, lifestyles, and so on which purport to demonstrate that the current organization of cities is not sustainable but can be made so if the correct measures are taken (Brand 2007). These measures often include actions aimed at influencing individual and collective behaviors and producing a new frame of reference for personal decision-making and conduct in everyday life, since changing lifestyles is considered as one of the enabling conditions for the environmental sustainability of smart cities (Yoshikawa et al. 2012). Thus, for instance, Nam and Pardo (2011) observe that transport policies should include references to healthy lifestyles and related concerns as a useful way of persuading citizens to change transport choices.

Persuading citizens to change their behaviors as a way to foster environmentally sustainable cities means asking them to 'participate' in making cities smarter, although this form of citizens' participation lies quite low on the Arnstein's ladder of participation. Indeed, when persuasion is pursued through the sharing of information (as it happens, for instance, when energy-providing companies provide customers with the energy usage information they need to change behavior patterns and reduce usage and costs), citizens' participation only reaches the bottom rung of the 'to-kenism' stage (Information). However, most often even this level is not achieved and policies for making cities environmentally sustainable simply 'manipulate' citizens or 'cure' them for their tendency to adopt non-sustainable behaviors. Citizens are pushed to embrace smart and sustainable behaviors by means of social regulation, sanction, inducement, exhortation and cajolery (Brand 2007). Through the manip-ulation of lifestyles towards green consumption, 'smartness' thus become a field of social control that, disguised as citizens' involvement and participation, makes intrusion in a person's private life quite natural (Vanolo 2014).

Consultation exercises are another example of possible disguised participation. Consultation is probably the most common form of citizens' participation in gov-ernment initiatives, including those aimed at making cities smarter. Actually, one meaning of a city's smartness is to reach a better knowledge of citizens' wants and needs and their opinions (Alawadhi et al. 2012), which could be done by consulting citizens. The smart city literature provides plenty of examples of initiatives involving citizens through a variety of tools and methods for consultation. These include both face-to-face events and surveys and the use of interactive technologies that allow the possibility to reach out to a much wider audience. The Local Action Plans developed within the EU funded PLACES project (http://www.openplaces.eu/resources/lap/) are examples of the use of different tools for citizens' engagement through consultation in sustainability related initiatives.

Web 2.0 tools (social networking services, social media or multimedia sharing, wikis, blogs, micro blogs and mash-ups) that provide channels not just for mass dissemination but also for mass consultation, production and collaboration (Linders 2012) are very useful tools for enabling participation through the sharing of information. Applied to community consultation, they allow citizens to share with government their understanding and perceptions of design, policy, and planning issues to achieve socially sustainable outcomes, which is one of the fundamental aims of smart city initiatives (Caldwell et al. 2013). This can lead to a new trend in the citizen-government relationship based on 'citizen sourcing' as a way to engage citizens in government related activities (Nam 2012).

Citizen sourcing is the process of gathering citizens' knowledge, ideas, opinions and needs in order to address various types of societal problems that government agencies face (Charalabidis et al. 2013). Through citizen sourcing, citizens are allowed to influence direction and outcomes, improve the government's situational awareness and even help execute government services on a day-to-day basis (Linders 2012), which enables forms of citizens' participation that can go well beyond simple consultation. However, as Linders (2012) points out, even in case citizen sourcing is resorted to as a way to engage citizens more directly in government related activities, government still holds the primary responsibility for them. How government exercises this responsibility determines the effectiveness of citizen sourcing as a public participation model.

According to Nam (2012), government can resort to citizen sourcing initiatives also for the purpose of 'image making', i.e., to increase public perception of government as being 'in touch' or 'social', readily able to react quickly to emerging technologies; reaching younger citizens and attracting the next generation of workers (p. 14). This use of citizen sourcing can be related to the information level of the Arnstein's classification or even to the manipulation level if the only aim is to enhance the citizenry's image of government.

Citizen-sourcing also fits other more serious purposes, for instance involving citizens as co-producers of knowledge and information, harnessing civic energies of citizens to solve public problems and promoting collaborative decision making processes (Nam 2012). When used with these purposes, citizen sourcing could enable forms of citizen participation that correspond to the higher levels of the Arnstein's ladder of participation, i.e. partnership, delegated power and even citizen control. However, to achieve these levels of participation the adoption and use of technological tools for citizen sourcing should be associated with a real re-distribution of power without which even using the more innovative tools for citizen participation does not lead beyond the level of placation.

If government agencies are not willing to actually consider and put into practice the results of a citizen sourcing exercise, it will seem like nothing more than rhetoric to citizen participants, which could undermine government-citizens relationships and may be counterproductive if citizens discover that their efforts and feedbacks have no impact or remain unaccounted (Nam 2012). The case of the Vancouver's 'EcoDensity' planning initiative described in (Rosol 2013) is a good example of the negative outcomes a consultation exercise conceived simply as a way to 'placate' citizens can have.

The risk that the results of a citizen sourcing exercise are not (cannot be) put into practice by government is quite likely to occur, as Schuurman et al. (2012) show with respect to idea generation and selection in smart cities through crowdsourcing. With reference to the results of a crowdsourcing exercise implemented by the city of Ghent (Belgium) as a first step in its smart city-strategy, Schuurman et al. observe that while offering significantly more user benefits than those suggested by (internal) professionals, the ideas and solutions suggested by users often are technically, legally or economically less feasible. Moreover, citizen-sourcing exercises might result in choices conflicting with the goals and policies of the city governments, which indicates a gap between the city and its citizens. This is a problem for city governments, but it could also be an opportunity if a genuine citizen-centric approach is assumed. Under such an approach, citizen sourcing could help city governments and policy makers to stay in touch with the citizens, one of the fundamental aspects in the process of cities becoming true smart cities (Schuurman et al. 2012). This, of course, at the condition that city governments and policy makers share power with citizens, which, in the cases considered in this section, means power to behave and to decide.

7.5   Citizens as Sensors/Information Providers

In this section a different form of citizens' participation will be considered that is
specific to smart cities, i.e. citizens participating in smart city initiatives as 'sensors'
providing information needed to implement them. The aim of the discussion is to
show what the re-balancing of the power relationships between government and
citizens could mean in this case.

As discussed in the previous section, the most obvious sense in which citizens
can be said to participate to the public life is by taking part in consultation exercises
supporting the city government in the decision-making and planning processes.
However, citizens can also participate to the implementation of public programs
and public services acting as co-implementers that make substantial resource
contributions to them, as it is usually required by true co-production relationships.
Bovaird (2007) describes some case studies in which citizens are actively involved
in the implementation of public initiatives, for instance acting as co-deliverers of
public services.

Citizens, as co-implementers, contribute to service production and delivery
through time, expertise and effort (Linders 2012), but also through compliance and
information (Alford 2009). Information is the most relevant resource citizens can
contribute to value co-production in the context of smart cities. The instrumentation
of smart cities (Harrison and Donnelly 2011) 'enables the capture and integration of
live real-world data through the use of sensors, kiosks, meters, personal devices,
appliances, cameras, smart phones, implanted medical devices, the web, and other
similar data-acquisition systems, including social networks as networks of human
sensors' (Chourabi et al. 2012, p. 2290). Such information is crucial for the
implementation of many services delivered by smart cities. Traditionally, this
information is collected through sensing and tracking infrastructures whose
implementation and maintenance is highly costly. An alternative way to collect data
across large cities is to exploit the potential of crowdsensing, i.e. by leveraging
information provided by sensors carried or set up by citizens.

The citizens' massive use of consumer-centric mobile sensing and computing
devices (such as smart phones and in-vehicle sensors) allows individuals to collectively share data and extract information to measure and map phenomena of
common interest. The intelligence and mobility of humans can thus be leveraged to
help applications to collect higher quality or semantically complex data that may
otherwise require sophisticated hardware and software (Ganti et al. 2011). This
gives rise to the so-called (Mobile) Crowdsensing trend that is primarily concerned
with data collection, processing, and interpretation and emphasizes the involvement
of users and community groups in social networks, documenting different aspects
of their lives (Mitton et al. 2012).

Like crowdsourcing, crowdsensing is a way to exploit the 'wisdom of the crowd'
(Surowiecki 2005). While crowdsourcing aims to leverage collective intelligence to
solve complex problems by splitting them in smaller tasks executed by the crowd,
crowdsensing splits the responsibility of harvesting information (typically urban

monitoring) to the crowd (Cardone et al. 2013). Citizens thus become sensors themselves (Goodchild 2007), providing the smart city with different types of information that can be used to better manage the city's systems, to implement user-centered services and to allow a better city experience for people. Acting as sensors, citizens enter in a relationship with the smart city's professionalized service providers making a substantial resource contribution (information), which according to Bovaird (2007) is the characteristic that defines co-production. Citizens as sensors/information providers can thus be considered as co-producers of the services they receive from the smart city.

Crowdsensing applications can be based on either 'participatory sensing' or 'opportunistic sensing' (Ganti et al. 2011). In general terms, participatory sensing applications use data from a mobile sensor node gathered in collaboration with its owner/operator (Burke et al. 2006). Hence, participatory sensing requires the active involvement of individuals to contribute data, for instance by taking pictures, reporting a road closure, sending information on traffic, etc. (Ganti et al. 2011). On the contrary, in the opportunistic sensing applications the data collection stage is fully automated with no user involvement; this lowers the burden placed on users (Lane et al. 2010) but increases the risk that users are unaware of the information being collected.

Both participatory and opportunistic sensing raise serious privacy concerns since crowdsensing applications could potentially collect sensitive data pertaining to individuals (Kapadia et al. 2009; Saroiu and Wolman 2010; Ganti et al. 2011). The risk of privacy breaches is not limited to the data collection phase; actually, the use of the collected data, which could also involve third parties, magnifies the risks for privacy since from the information collected from citizens as sensors, personal data and personal information can be extracted directly or through further processing. From this point of view, the resource that citizens as sensors provide to the smart city ultimately involves personal data (including in this category also the data generated by the citizens' behaviors).

Personal information represents a valuable resource increasingly recognized as the new 'oil' of the 21st century (WEF 2011), an important currency in the new millennium to which also a relevant monetary value can be associated (Thaler et al. 2013). Hence, acting as sensors/information providers in smart city initiatives, citizens not only assume a risk concerning possible threats to their privacy but also provide the smart city with a highly valuable resource.

Most often, citizens act as unconscious sensors that unconsciously provide information to fuel smart cities. When walking along a street or moving inside a parking, citizens are seldom completely aware of the fact that their image is taken by security cameras and stored for security reasons, even if the presence of cameras is properly signaled. People are very unlikely to be aware of the information that smart meters acquire and of how this information can be used, by whom and with which aims (Molina-Markham et al. 2010; EDPS 2012). Similarly, when posting a message on Twitter or uploading pictures on Flickr people are not aware that this information could be used by a third party to extract further information that can be used in ways people as the source of information is completely unaware of (Villatoro et al. 2012; Sagl et al. 2012).

Collecting information from unconscious citizens acting as sensors/information providers reduces citizens' participation to a form of manipulation. Informing citizens that data generated by their behaviors are collected, how this is done and for what aims, is a way to make citizens more conscious of their role as information providers. However, simply asking citizens the permission to collect their data, as it usually happens when people are required to agree on the terms stated in End User License Agreements (EULA), it is not enough since, as observed above, the major problems for privacy come from the use of personal data by organizations, not simply from their collection (Mundie 2014). Without giving citizens control over the way their personal data are used, and will be used, asking them the permission to collect their data simply amounts to a form of placation, which is still something pertaining more to the rhetoric of participation than to true participation.

What are then the conditions that would allow citizens acting as sensors/information providers to participate as partners in smart cities initiatives? Considered as a form of participation, partnership requires the establishment of an equal and reciprocal relationship with the service providers, which enables citizens to negotiate and engage in trade-offs with the traditional service providers (the power-holders) (Arnstein 1969). The fundamental condition enabling the establishment of such an equal and reciprocal relationship is the rebalancing of the power-relationship between citizens and service providers. However, what could this mean when citizens participate in smart city initiatives as sensors/information providers?

Personal data are not simply data concerning an individual but, more generally, information identifiable to the individual (Kang 1998—citing the Clinton Administration's Information Infrastructure Task Force), which includes information that can be related to an individual because she/he generated it. As data producers, citizens could claim an ownership right on the data related to them and claim to control the terms under which such information is acquired, disclosed, and used, which is what information privacy amounts to (Kang 1998). Personal data ownership, i.e. 'who owns the data' and 'what rights does ownership imply', is still an open question, mainly due to the difficulty of extending to data the traditional property rights (Schwartz 2004; WEF 2011). For instance, it is still widely discussed whether an individual has the right of selling his personal data or whether privacy is an inalienable right. Even without entering the complexities of the discussion on personal data ownership, it is quite reasonable to claim that citizens should be given some form of control over the data they generate with their behaviors, both in the real world and online. Hence, instead of 'Who owns user-generated (personal) data?' the question to consider is 'Who controls user-generated data?'

In the today personal data landscape, an asymmetry of power exists between organizations and individuals due to an asymmetry in the amount of information about individuals held by, or that is accessible to, organizations, and the lack of knowledge and ability of individuals to control the use of that information (WEF

2011). This asymmetry is reflected in the traditional organization centric model for personal data management. Under this model, user-generated data are collected by organizations that store them in their IT systems. By agreeing on the terms and conditions defined by the organizations that collect their user-generated data, individuals delegate to the data collectors the protection of their data. It is then expected that the data collectors will manage the data according to security and privacy policies that comply with the existing legislation, and using the appropriate data-protection techniques (such as encryption, data perturbation, anonymization, pseudonymization and tokenization). Thus, in the organization-centric model for personal data management, the collectors of information exert on the user-generated data much more control than the individuals who generated it. This makes the rebalancing of the power relationship between citizens as information providers and service providers (who use citizen-generated data to implement the services) hardly compatible with the organization-centric model for personal data management.

The continuous technological evolution that made low cost information management tools for gathering, storing and sharing information available to individuals and the exponential growth of the intensity of personal data processing are creating today the conditions for the emergence of a new paradigm for personal data management, based on a user-centric view, alternative to the traditional organization-centric view. In the user-centric paradigm (Moiso and Minerva 2012; Cavoukian 2013), individuals are considered as the 'owners' of the data they generate; hence, individuals should be allowed to exert a higher control over the whole lifecycle of their personal data. This would allow citizens also to decide whether to disclose their data to trusted organizations in order to receive some useful services from them.

The raising of the user-centric paradigm is being enabled also by some international trends. At the level of regulation, the European Commission's proposal for the reform of the data protection rules assumes as its objective to give citizens back control over their personal data (EU 2007). At the level of governments, some programs are being implemented that aim at the same objective. The UK Government initiative 'Midata' that encourages companies to release the data they hold on citizens (as customers) back to the them, thereby empowering them as managers of their own data (BIS 2014), is an example of an initiative targeted to the private sector. Another example, directly involving government, is the 'Blue Button' initiative in the USA that allows veterans to download a copy of their health data (WEF 2011). At the level of economy, the World Economic Forum launched the project 'Rethinking Personal Data' to drive new thinking on how governments and industry can create new economic and social value from personal data through the active involvement of individuals as the data owners (WEF 2011).

Why, however, citizens would be willing to share their data once they have given back control over them? A possible answer to this question can be found by considering the attitude of citizens as consumers towards the companies that collect their data for commercial purposes. A survey conducted in November 2014 among over 2000 U.S. adults ages 18+ shows that the majority of consumers (67 % of the sample) would be willing to give companies access to much of their personal information if they would get better, more personalized services/products in return (Transera 2014). Hence, even when it could be expected that their privacy concerns are high (i.e. when they interact with companies as consumers) citizens are nevertheless willing to share (at least some of) their personal data if this brings them some benefits. When such benefits directly concern them (for instance discounts or better consumer experience in a co-production relation with sellers), citizens have the opportunity of evaluating the trade-off between privacy and utility and, on this basis, to increase or decrease the level of trust and the willingness to allow an organization to use their data. This clearly shows that if citizens are given the possibility of taking control over their data and evaluating the trade-off between the risk of privacy breaches and expected or perceived benefits they could act as conscious and collaborative information providers, thus improving the quality of the co-production relationship.

In the context of smart cities, giving the citizens back control over their data would give them the power to decide whether to allow the smart city to collect and use them, based on the evaluation of the trade-off between privacy concerns and expected benefits. Smart cities can deliver many benefits to their citizens, also in terms of utilities for them (i.e. a private value). However, initiatives aimed at making cities smarter are usually intended to create also other elements of value-added, for instance environmental sustainability, social inclusion or the spreading of benefits across the widest possible range of local community members. Hence, the value citizens would receive back as a compensation for allowing smart cities to collect and use their data is not only a value for them, but also possibly a value for the wider population and for future generations of citizens as well, i.e. a public value. From this point of view, public value is a fundamental component of the evaluation of the trade-off between the risk of privacy breaches and expected benefits that, once they have been given back the control over their user-generated data, would make citizens conscious and informed data providers acting as co-producers and partners in the development of smart cities.

7.6 Conclusions and Further Research Directions

In this chapter, some aspects of citizens' participation in smart city initiatives have been discussed as a way for citizens to contribute their 'smartness' to make cities smarter. The discussion has been based on the Arnstein's principle according to which there cannot be true participation without the rebalancing of the power relationship between the power-holders (city governments and professional public service providers) and the have-nots (citizens). By reference to the literature on public services co-production, the concept of co-production has been assumed to explain what citizens' participation can amount to when based on a more balanced power relationship between service providers and service users. Using Arnstein's description of participation and the concept of co-production as the lens through which to consider citizens' participation in smart city initiatives, it has been shown how participation exercises risk to be little more than rhetoric if some real power is not given back to citizens. What this means depends on the domain in which the participation exercise is implemented, since having the power to express preferences, the power to decide or the power to act are quite different things.

The chapter considered in some details the role that citizens can play as sensors/information providers, which is a role quite specific to smart cities initiatives. In fact, citizens can participate in initiatives aimed at making cities smarter by providing information that can be used by the city's government and by the professional service providers to better manage the city's systems, to implement user-centered services and to allow a better city experience for people. Most of this information is generated by citizens' behaviors and, as such, it directly pertains to them, at the point that citizens could claim the right to control it. In the chapter, it has been argued that giving back to citizens the control over the information pertaining to them is the condition that, by rebalancing the power relationship between government (and professional service providers) and citizens, enables citizens to participate in the development of smart cities as 'smart' service co-producers.

This could seem a quite obvious, and even trivial, claim. However, it is not obvious at all if we consider what its far-reaching implications could be. As observed above, giving back to citizens the control over the user-generated information allows them to decide whether and how to share this resource with the city's government and the professional service providers, based on a cost–benefit calculation. Citizens would thus be allowed to decide to play a co-producer role for those services from which the higher benefit for them can be expected, and not for the services that the city's government and the service providers presume are the most useful for citizens. This would force city's governments and service providers to go beyond the vendor push and technological driven approach that still seems dominant in the smart city scenario worldwide to assume a truly citizen-centric approach instead.

Giving back to citizens the control over the data they generate has another important implication for the relationship between citizens and government. In a user-centric personal data ecosystem, citizens can decide to share their user-generated data not only with governments but also with other subjects (organizations, communities, individuals) that could use them to implement services that citizens appraise. Although they are typically designed without any input from governments and have users/communities as the service deliverers, such user-generated services can nevertheless deliver a public value to citizens. As such, they should be included within the public sphere and, hence, be considered as user-generated public services. Giving back to them the control over the data they generate is thus a way to empower citizens, which is one of the conditions enabling the emergence of the so-called user-generated state (or state 2.0), as the result of the transformation of public administration in the digital era.

Of course, there are many problems that must be solved and further research is needed before the above-mentioned possibilities can be turned into reality. In fact, the development of a user-centric personal information ecosystem, which is an enabling condition for the users' control over the data they generate, raises many serious problems that have not been discussed in the chapter. Such problems concern the technological level (the definition of new architectures and new systems allowing users to manage their data in a secure and efficient way), the organization level (the redefinition of the organizations' data management systems) and the legal level as well (the definition of a new regulation on personal data).

Moreover, giving citizens the power to share their user-generated data based on a cost-benefit calculation raises also the problem of what should be evaluated and how citizens can perform the evaluation. As observed above, public value provides a better explanation of the citizens' willingness to participate in public initiatives than purely selfish motivation. From this point of view, the cost-benefit calculation should include public value as a fundamental component beside the value for them (i.e., a private value) that citizens expect from the services delivered to them. However, a public value-based evaluation entails a new conceptualization of citizens, different from the view of citizens as 'clients' typical of the New Public Management approach that has been dominant in the public management literature during the past decades, and that still appears to be dominant in many smart city conceptualizations.

To allow citizens to perform a sound cost-benefit calculation that includes also public value, citizens should have all the information required to evaluate the outputs, outcomes and impacts of public initiatives. This requires governments to implement systems for the evaluation of public initiatives (which is seldom done, also due to the high costs for evaluation) and to share the results of the evaluation exercises with citizens in a transparent way. Moreover, since the evaluation should be public value-based, new concepts, frameworks, models and tools have to be developed quite different from those used in the more traditional and mainly efficiency-based evaluation of the results achieved by public initiatives.

Despite all these problems, giving back to citizens the control over their user-generated data still appears as the fundamental condition that would allow citizens to participate actively in smart city initiatives as sensors/information providers. Although limited only to one of the many roles citizens can play in smart city initiatives, the discussion of this chapter gives a further example of how citizens can provide their smartness to make cities smarter, as long as they are given power enough to act as true co-producers.

References

S. Alawadhi, et al., Building Understanding of Smart City Initiatives, in *Electronic Government. 11th IFIP WG 8.5 International Conference*, ed. by H.J. Scholl, M. Janssen, M. Wimmer, C. Moe, L. Flak. Kristiansand, September 2012. Lecture Notes in Computer Science, vol. 7443 (Springer, Berlin, 2012), p. 40

J. Alford, *Public Sector Clients: From Service-Delivery to Co-production* (Palgrave Macmillan, Basingstoke, 2009)

S. Arnstein, The ladder of citizen participation. J. Am. I. Planners **35**, 216–224 (1969)

B. Baccarne, P. Mechant, D. Schuurman, Empowered Cities? An Analysis of the Structure and Generated Value of the Smart City Ghent, in *Smart City*, ed. by R.P. Dameri, C. Rosenthal-Sabroux (Springer, Berlin, 2014), pp. 157–182

J. Belissent, *Getting Clever about Smart Cities: New Opportunities Require New Business Models* (Forrester Research, Cambridge, 2010)

J. Benington, From Private Choice to Public Value?, in *Public Value: Theory and practice*, ed. by J. Benington, M. Moore (Palgrave Macmillan, Basingstoke, 2011), pp. 31–51

BIS, *Personal Data—Review of the Midata Voluntary Programme* (Department for Business, Innovation & Skills, London, 2014)

T. Bovaird, Beyond engagement and participation: user and community coproduction of public services. Public Admin Rev **67**, 846–860 (2007)

T. Bovaird, E. Loeffler, From engagement to co-production: the contribution of users and communities to outcomes and public value. Voluntas **23**, 1119–1138 (2012)

P. Brand, Green subjection: the politics of neoliberal Urban environmental management. Int. J. Urban Reg. **31**, 616–632 (2007)

J. Burke, et al., Participatory Sensing, in *Proceedings of the ACM Sensys World Sensor Web Workshop* (Boulder, 2006)

G.A. Caldwell, M. Foth, M. Guaralda, An urban informatics approach to smart city learning in architecture and urban design education. IxD&A **17**, 7–28 (2013)

G. Cardone et al., Fostering participation in smart cities: a geo-social crowdsensing platform. IEEE Commun. Mag. **51**, 112–119 (2013)

L. Carter, F. Bélanger, The utilization of e-government services: citizen trust, innovation and acceptance factors. J. Inf. Syst. **15**, 5–25 (2005)

A. Cavoukian, Personal Data Ecosystem (PDE)—A Privacy by Design Approach to an Individual's Pursuit of Radical Control, in *Digital Enlightenment Yearbook 2013*, ed. by M. Hildebrandt, et al. (IOS Press, Amsterdam, 2013), pp. 89–101

Y. Charalabidis et al., Requirements and Architecture of a Passive Crowdsourcing Environment, in *Electronic Government and Electronic Participation—Joint Proceedings of Ongoing Research of IFIP EGOV and ePart 2013, Koblenz, September 2013*, ed. by M.A. Wimmer, M. Janssen, A. Macintosh, H.J. Scholl, E. Tambouris (Gesellschaft für Informatik, Bonn, 2013), pp. 208–217

H. Chourabi, et al., Understanding Smart Cities: An Integrative Framework, in *Proceedings of the 45th Hawaii International Conference on System Sciences* (HICCS 2012) (IEEE Press, Maui, 2012), pp. 2289–2297

A. Cornwall, Unpacking 'participation': Models, meanings, and practices. Community Dev. J. **43**, 269–283 (2008)

E. Cosgrave, T. Tryfonas, T. Crick, The Smart City from a Public Value Perspective, in *Proceedings of the 2nd International Conference on ICT for Sustainability* (ICT4S 2014) (Stockholm, 2014), pp. 369–377

M. Deakin, From Intelligent to Smart Cities, in *Smart Cities: Governing, Modelling and Analysing the Transition*, ed. by M. Deakin (Routledge, London, 2013), pp. 15–32

S. Dirks, M. Keeling, *A Vision of Smarter Cities—How Cities can Lead the Way into a Prosperous and Sustainable Future* (IBM Institute for Business Value, 2009)

EDPS, Opinion of the Data Protection Supervisor. (European Data Protection Supervisor, 2012). www.edps.europa.eu/EDPSWEB/webdav/site/mySite/shared/Documents/Consultation/Opinions/2012/12-06-08_Smart_metering_EN.pdf. Accessed 3 Jan 2016

M. Etgar, A descriptive model of the consumer co-production process. J. Acad. Market Sci. **36**, 97–108 (2008)

EU, Opinion 4/2007 on the concept of personal data. Article 29 Data Protection Working Party—01248/07/EN WP 136. (European Commission, Brussels, 2007)

A. Fung, Varieties of participation in complex governance. Public Admin. Rev. **66**, 66–75 (2006)

G. Galdon-Clavell, (Not so) smart cities?: The drivers, impact and risks of surveillance enabled smart environments. Sci. Public Policy **40**, 717–723 (2013)

R.K. Ganti, F. Ye, H. Lei, Mobile crowdsensing: current state and future challenges. IEEE Commun. Mag. **49**, 32–39 (2011)

R. Gauld, S. Goldfinch, S. Horsburgh, Do they want it? Do they use it? The 'Demand-Side' of e-Government in Australia and New Zealand. Gov. Inform. Q. **27**, 177–186 (2010)

R. Giffinger, et al., *Smart Cities: Ranking of European Medium-Sized Cities* (Centre of Regional Science (SRF), Vienna University of Technology, 2007). http://www.smartcities.eu/download/smart_cities_final_report.pdf. Accessed 3 Jan 2016

J.R. Gil-García, T.A. Pardo, e-Government success factors: mapping practical tools to theoretical foundations. Gov. Inform. Q. **22**, 187–216 (2005)

M. Goodchild, Citizens as sensors: the world of volunteered geography. GeoJournal **69**, 211–221 (2007)

J.T. Gourville, *Why Consumers Don't Buy: The Psychology of New Product Adoption* (Harvard Business School Note #504–056, 2004)

C. Harrison, I.A. Donnelly, A Theory of Smart Cities, in*Proceedings of the 55th Annual Meeting of the International Society for the Systems Sciences* (University of Hull Business School, 2011), pp. 521–535

J. Hartley, Public Value through Innovation and Improvement, in *Public Value: Theory and practice*, ed. by J. Benington, M. Moore (Palgrave Macmillan, Basingstoke, 2011), pp. 171–184

J.M. Hernandez-Munoz, et al., Smart Cities at the Forefront of the Future Internet, in *The Future Internet*, ed. by J. Domingue, A. Galis, A. Gavras, T. Zahariadis, et al. (Springer, Berlin, 2011) pp. 447–462

R. Hollands, Critical interventions into the corporate smart city. Camb. J. Reg. Econ. Soc. **8**, 61–77 (2015)

ITU, *Smart Sustainable Cities—Analysis of Definitions* (International Telecommunication Union, Focus Group on Smart and Sustainable Cities, 2014). SSC-0100-rev-3

J. Kang, Information privacy in cyberspace transactions. Stanford Law Rev. **50**, 1193–1294 (1998)

A. Kapadia, D. Kotz, N. Triandopoulos, Opportunistic Sensing: Security Challenges for the New Paradigm, in *Proceedings of COMSNETS 2009. The First International Conference on COMunication Systems and NETworks* (Bangalore, 2009), pp. 127–136

M. Kunstelj, M. Vintar, Evaluating the progress of e-government development: a critical analysis. Inform. Polity **9**, 131–148 (2004)

N. Lane et al., A survey of mobile phone sensing. IEEE Commun. Mag. **48**, 140–150 (2010)

D. Linders, From e-government to we-government: defining a typology for citizen coproduction in the age of social media. Gov. Inform. Q. **29**, 446–454 (2012)

P. Lombardi et al., An Analytic Network Model for Smart Cities, in *Proceedings of the 11th International Symposium on the Analytic Hierarchy Process*, ed. by F. de Felice, A. Petrillo (Sorrento, 2011)

N. Mitton et al., Combining Cloud and sensors in a smart city environment. EURASIP J. Wirel. Commun. Netw. **247**, 1–10 (2012)

C. Moiso, R. Minerva, Towards a User-Centric Personal Data Ecosystem. The Role of the Bank of Individuals' Data, in *Proceedings of the 16th International Conference on Intelligence in Next Generation Networks* (ICIN) (Berlin, 2012), pp. 202–209

A. Molina-Markham et al., Private Memoirs of a Smart Meter, in *Proceedings of the 2nd ACM Workshop on Embedded Sensing Systems for Energy-Efficiency in Buildings* (BuildSys 2010) (Zurich, 2010), pp. 61–66

C. Mundie, Privacy pragmatism. Foreign Aff. 39 (2014)

T. Nam, Suggesting frameworks of citizen-sourcing via Government 2.0. Gov. Inform. Q. **29**, 12–20 (2012)

T. Nam, T. Pardo, Smart City as Urban Innovation: Focusing on Management, Policy, and Context, in *Proceedings of the 5th International Conference on Theory and Practice of Electronic Governance (ICEGOV 2011)*, ed. by E. Estevez, M. Janssen, (Tallinn, 2011), pp. 185–194

P. Neirotti et al., Current trends in smart city initiatives: some stylised facts. Cities **38**, 25–36 (2014)

W. Olphert, L. Damodaran, Citizen participation and engagement in the design of egovernment services: the missing link in effective ICT design and delivery. J. Assoc. Inf. Sys. **8**, 491–507 (2007)

C.K. Prahalad, V. Ramaswamy, Co-creation experiences: the next practice in value creation. J. Interact. Mark **18**, 5–14 (2004)

C.G. Reddick, Citizen interaction with e-government: from the streets to servers? Gov. Inform. Q. **22**, 38–57 (2005)

M. Rosol, Vancouver's "Ecodensity" planning initiative: a struggle over hegemony? Urban Stud. **50**, 2238–2255 (2013)

G. Rowe, L. Frewer, A typology of public engagement mechanisms. Sci. Technol. Hum. Val. **30**, 251–290 (2005)

G. Sagl et al., From Social Sensor Data to Collective Human Behaviour Patterns: Analysing and Visualising SpatioTemporal Dynamics in Urban Environments, in *GI_Forum 2012: Geovizualisation, Society and Learning*, ed. by T. Jekel, A. Car, J. Strobl, G. Griesebner (Herbert Wichmann Verlag, Berlin, 2012)

S. Saroiu, A. Wolman, I am a Sensor, and I Approve this Message,in *Proceedings of the 11th Workshop on Mobile Computing Systems and Applications (HotMobile 2010)* (Annapolis, 2010), pp. 37–42

H. Schaffers et al., Smart Cities and the Future Internet: Towards Cooperation Frameworks for Open Innovation, in *The Future Internet*, ed. by J. Domingue, et al. (Springer, Berlin, 2011), pp. 431–446

D. Schuurman et al., Smart ideas for smart cities: investigating crowdsourcing for generating and selecting ideas for ICT innovation in a city context. J. Theor. Appl. Electron. Commer. Res. **7**, 49–62 (2012)

P. Schwartz, Property, privacy, and personal data. Harvard Law Rev. **117**, 2056–2128 (2004)

E. Sharp, Toward a new understanding of Urban services and citizen participation: the co-production concept. Midwest Rev. Public Adm. **14**, 105–118 (1980)

H. Standing, *Understanding the 'Demand Side' in Service Delivery. Definition, Frameworks and Tools* (UK Department of International Development, London, 2004)

J. Surowiecki, *The Wisdom of Crowds: Why the Many Are Smarter Than the Few and How Collective Wisdom Shapes Business, Economies, Societies and Nations* (Doubleday Knopf Publisher, New York, 2005)

R.H. Thaler, W. Tucker, Smarter information, smarter consumers. Harvard Bus Rev. 45–54 (2013)

Transera, Survey Research Results: Consumer Perceptions about Big Data and its Benefis. White Paper (2014). www.transerainc.com. Accessed 3 Jan 2016

J.Q. Tritter, A. McCallum, The snakes and ladders of user involvement: moving beyond Arnstein. Health Policy **76**, 156–168 (2006)

A. Vanolo, Smartmentality: the smart city as disciplinary strategy. Urban Stud. **51**, 883–898 (2014)

P. Verdegem, G. Verleye, User-centered e-government in practice: a comprehensive model for measuring user satisfaction. Gov. Inform. Q. **26**, 487–497 (2009)

D. Villatoro, M. Pus, M. Torrent-Moreno, Citizen as a Sensor: The Barcelona Urban Mobility Use-case, in *Proceedings of the Smart City Expo World Congress* (Barcelona, 2012)

WEF, *Personal Data: The Emergence of a New Asset Class* (World Economic Forum, Cologny, 2011)

G. Whitaker, Co-production: citizen participation in service delivery. Public Admin. Rev. **40**, 240–246 (1980)

Y. Yoshikawa et al., Hitachi's vision of the smart city. Hitachi Rev. **61**, 111–118 (2012)

Chapter 8
The Role of ICT in Co-Production of e-Government Public Services

Mariagrazia Fugini and Mahsa Teimourikia

8.1 Introduction

Recent developments in ICT have raised the interest of different Countries in service provisioning from public organizations, for short called "e-Government function". In fact, ICT and e-Government has since long been considered an important strategy of administration and transformation of the relationship among government, citizens and companies on a given territory.

On the other side, co-production is growing as a paradigm. In the literature, there exist various definitions of co-production, each capturing a dimension of its meaning, as illustrated in Chap. 1. *Co-production of e-Government services* can be defined as any active behavior by anyone, outside the government agencies, able to create private/public value on a voluntary basis, and in collaboration with, or independently of, the government agencies (Alford 2009). More precisely, co-production in e-Government refers to the involvement of users in knowledge generation within knowledge-intensive services (Bettencourt et al. 2005).

In this chapter, we consider co-production as the paradigm representing the *involvement and collaboration of end users in improving the services of E-Government applications*. It turns out that managers, private and public organizations, and individuals or communities can be highly involved not only as consumers, but also as decision makers in the service provisioning phase and during the whole life cycle of services.

As a general concept, in all the fields of society, and in e-Government alike, the need for more effective *Information Systems (ISs)* arises. ISs are systems of *data* and *procedures* executing (business) *processes*. More and more the need arises to involve users and stakeholders in the development, and maintenance of those *processes and data*, which constitute the *output and outcome* of the IS, namely

M. Fugini (✉) · M. Teimourikia
Polytechnic of Milan, Milano, Italy
e-mail: mariagrazia.fugini@polimi.it

© The Author(s) 2016   119
M. Fugini et al. (eds.), *Co-production in the Public Sector*,
PoliMI SpringerBriefs, DOI 10.1007/978-3-319-30558-5_8

services, in a way that encourages co-production and participation, feedback, and verification of the system functionalities by diverse user communities and territories covered by the IS. Nowadays, an IS is intended as an automated, ICT-based distributed system of hardware, software (applications and databases) and telecommunications components, able to process large quantities of *information* and to *orchestrate different business processes* (Laudon and Laudon 2011). An IS can operate in many different areas: from manufacturing, to supply chain management, from e-commerce to provisioning of *public services* (e.g., health, social care, employment, administration services).

In particular, the requirements of *public services* pose a never-stopping request for more effective development tools for ISs, such as agile ICT platforms for development and provisioning of services, as well as methods for developing and using services with the cooperation of users in a co-production style, from the early concept stages.

This chapter is organized as follows. Section 8.2 presents co-production in e-Government services. Section 8.3 presents the first case study, namely *services for employment*. Section 8.4 illustrates the second case study, namely *services for integrated health and social care* (Fugini et al. 2014, 2015). Section 8.5 overviews emerging products and paradigms in ICT. Section 8.6 draws the conclusions.

8.2 E-Government and Co-production

The term *e-Government* represents the idea of an improvement of efficiency and effectiveness in government functions by *Public Administrations* (*PAs*). However, e-Government still seems to have a long way ahead before becoming a true *tool of governance,* since, there are many issues and barriers, including barriers on the technical aspects and the use of new ICT, barriers between government and citizens, and, in addition, barriers regarding cultural and structural aspects (Meijer 2015).

ICT is currently massively present in PAs to support both *administrative functions* and to provide *added value services* for citizens, enterprises, and organizations, although simply favouring customized and updated knowledge, and eventually to provide *government functions*. Moreover, recent advancements in ICT, such as social media, web 2.0, Internet of Things, big and open data, and security and privacy, play an important role in empowering users and citizens co-production in playing an active role in the functioning of a government through e-Government services (Linders 2012).

To achieve co-production in e-Government services and applications, the following aspects should be considered (Fugini et al. 2014):

- Involving the stakeholders and users from the start.
- Finding ways to reward anyone who takes part in co-production.
- Since the budget for e-Government services can be limited, the costs for incorporating co-production should be reduced, not forgetting that co-production can

inherently lead to cost reduction, since voluntary citizens can handle many tasks rather than involving only experts, who are paid for their work.

- Providing the means of easy-to-use and accessible communication for everyone. In this way, co-producers can easily interact with cooperating entities.
- Since citizens come from many backgrounds, cultures, education, and so on, the ICT platforms designed for co-production should consider these diversities and be understandable also for non-technical users.
- ICT platforms of services needed for co-production should be built on top of the existing e-Government platforms to avoid extra costs and time for re-implementing the old ones.
- Information sharing and knowledge management play an important role in co-production as the needed information should be available to co-producers, and for decision-making.
- Co-producers should be able to report problems, send feedbacks, and be involved in communities and forums where they can state their opinions, and the data gathered in this way can be used in improvements of functionalities and services.
- Citizens and users involved in co-production should receive proper training to be able to perform their tasks correctly.
- Organizational and administrative authorities should make sure that the involved people are competent and have the capacity to be involved in co-production.
- Gaining the peoples trust in e-Government by protecting their privacy to encourage their participation in co-production.

To understand the evolution of e-Government around society, and the ways to incorporate co-production in government functionalities, the issues and barriers need to be studied.

Social media play an important role in today's e-Government initiatives and provide innovative ways for budget-strapped governments to incorporate co-production using the massive resources of low-cost social media to involve citizens in delivering public value (Linders 2012). Yet, aspects such as security and privacy should be considered in the development stages of e-Government services to ensure that citizens' trust in e-Government remains intact.

ICT advances adopted in e-Government are means to facilitate co-production. However, risks regarding security of information due to shared data arise, which threaten the privacy of different involved entities, and this is a barrier. Moving from traditional non-digital channels for government procedures to the web introduces many security and privacy challenges, while also increasing the costs of protecting the resources at risk. Furthermore, different entities sharing data and knowledge might have diverse security and privacy policies.

Another issue is the outsourcing of critical information to external corporations that on a dark side might have no regard for the right for privacy and misuse information for electronic surveillance. Therefore, a strategy should be developed to consider a common basis for defining unique and uniform security and privacy policies that guarantee the confidentiality, integrity, and availability of shared knowledge. In (Jaafar et al. 2014), authors propose a model for securing services of e-Government that involves the registration, verification, and certification of different entities that access e-Government services. However, security and privacy of e-Government services encompass many open issues since a balance is needed between restrictions and ease-of-use, quick services (with low burdens which for instance cryptography brings about) and open access to services.

Moreover, it is of outmost importance to evaluate the trustworthiness of the different entities collaborating in providing the services and the development of e-Government (Colesca 2015). Since in co-production and e-governance outsourcing and cooperation of different entities are the basis to gather data, share skills, and so on, there is the need to examine the trustworthiness of these entities. Trust model development has to consider various criteria to evaluate the level of trust, including the history of previous collaborations, the reputation of involved entities, social rankings on trust and reputation, or the importance and criticality of the produced results, and so on. The trust model, however, should be incorporated by all involved sub-organizations that collaborate with each other, to be able to apply a unique and global definition of trust.

ICT can be an effective paradigm for reducing vulnerabilities and obstacles in face of incorporating co-production in e-Government services, which instead is often perceived as an obstacle or a burden. Adopting the most up-to-date technology is an opportunity for developing new services, which are understood and participated upon from the early stages of introduction by all the involved actors, including those in non-technical roles. For example, end users of health or employment services can provide their own requirements in front of a new technology, e.g., a service provided via wearable devices, and can themselves become the supporters of acceptance while shortening the times and costs of ICT introduction and of perception of the benefits.

8.3 Case Study: Services for Employment

In e-Government, an example of co-production is offered by services for employment, offered to prevent unemployment through an ICT based network (web) of functions for citizens, companies, and public and private job operators. ISs for Employment are called *Employment Information Systems* (*EIS*) in the sequel. Since employment has a high impact on a person's life, such as carrier, life style and work satisfaction, besides financial support, co-production of these services can be helpful when private and public agencies get the end user opinions and help in defining such services.

One basic issue is that *human capital* is the key factor of economic growth and of competitiveness in the information age and knowledge economy. However, due to a fragmented employment market pressed by globalization and by the rules and laws, human resources are not effectively exchanged and deployed.

e-Government plans in Europe have been centered also on building *European systems that provide services* used *for job placement, personal education* and *qualification*. Advances in ICT can overcome many of the limitations present in national and international systems, such as low data circulation, scarce interoperability, and heterogeneity both at the administrative level of norms and classifications adopted (e.g., in the job placement domain) and at the technological level.

If traditionally the employment market has been mostly a prerogative of specialized entities (private/public employment agencies, recruiting and job search companies), its social implications and enormous impact onto the political/strategic decisions of governments have seen an increasing implication of National and Local PAs. ICT can improve the effectiveness and efficiency of the relationship of government with citizens, private companies and employment agencies.

Two employment systems, SOC and BLL, are examples in the area of this use case. These systems are discussed since we cooperated directly in their development. Moreover, they operate in two European Regions, which are very similar from a social/cultural and economic viewpoints but perform differently. One reason of the different performance is related, in our opinion, to co-production: SOC was created using a bottom up design, starting from user-developed systems, while BLL followed a top down development, which took the user inputs to a limited or even no consideration.

8.3.1 Servei D'Ocupació de Catalunya (SOC)

SOC is an EIS of the Department of Job of the Government of Catalonia. A free guidance public service offers a job intermediation function between job seekers and companies. The service also offers career and training. Services provided through the website initially included only renewal of job applications and benefits management for unemployed people. Then, these services evolved to support a real marketplace.

Co-production of services for employment is facilitated through SOC thanks to its interconnections with private systems such as InfoJobs or Monster. The website's usability, layout and vocabulary are fit for the purpose, engaging users, and making it easy to use and understand the system's functions for non-technical citizens. Furthermore, digital certification to access the website services ensures privacy and security, granting the citizens trust about their data privacy. Nevertheless, SOC is undergoing the development of further functions improving the quality of services. Moreover, systems exist grounded on public initiatives and external to SOC, e.g., Porta22 promoted by Barcelona City Council, that provide one of the main elements of co-production in this system, that concerns young people and long-term unemployed people, offering professional guidance, with educational services offered in classrooms. These activities, promoted by public administrations, are provided on a voluntary basis.

Community-promoted initiatives are supported by independent organizations and so it is difficult to include their ISs in an integrated system, due to different data structures and processes.

8.3.2 Borsa Lavoro Lombardia (BLL)

The BLL portal of the Lombard Regional Administration is an EIS for integrated access to services for job, education and training, creating a network of services where operators, individuals and companies can meet in a cooperative (web-based) environment. BLL is a distributed EIS, based on the technology of web services, so that no modifications to the connected systems are required. The aim is exchanging information about CVs and job offers on a wide territory, supporting also *private intermediaries* of the labour market (e.g. temporary work agency, job placement agencies) and end-users, namely job seekers and companies.

Through BLL, users can access several informative and interactive areas regarding *employment*, *education* and *training*. This is a key vehicle for information and data exchange, and a support to interaction between Citizens and Companies.

Unlike SOC, BLL does not consider citizen co-production in providing training for job seekers as it incorporates training courses organized by public and private organizations. However, BLL incorporates co-production by offering services such as an area for personal opinions, discussions, questions and informative requests. These can be used as the platform where citizens can take the role of experts in discussions to answer the questions of their peers and to guide them using their experiences, and to gather the public feedback and reports on the issues needing considerations.

BLL considers privacy of users in the platform by hiding the contact information from the companies who are searching for workforce. Furthermore, a combination of provisioning of information and interactive services modes, accessible using multi-channel technology, guarantees unified access, sustains the merging of local systems and private systems into a shared network, promotes the exchange of information from/ to the integrated system present in the labour market and some links to other regional and international bodies.

8.3.3 Observations

The *dimensions of service provisioning* assess the quality of the services offered by e-Government in both systems, SOC and BLL. We have analyzed these dimensions, although benefits of e-Government programs cannot be calculated only in financial and economic terms because the implementation of projects can lead to improvements in access to services or the quality of the information provided (reduction in waiting times, timeliness of information access, etc.). The sub-dimensions are service quality, satisfaction and fulfillment and the usefulness of information provided. The *social dimension*, which involves co-production, is a key factor in model evaluation for public administrations. Sub-dimensions are fairness of service provision (including security, justice, etc.), trust and confidence in government (including transparency, accountability, security, privacy, etc.) and satisfaction regarding human development (including learning, skills, health, etc.). The *political and democratic dimension*, although including social aspects, is also related to openness, transparency, accountability, and participation. Openness refers to policy drafts available and processes open online; transparency and accountability refers to processes traceable online and agencies reporting their expenditure online; and participation refers to contributions to online forums and queries submitted online. The analyzed dimensions that we propose are presented in Table 8.1.

In order to validate the proposed indicators for the assessment and benchmarking of public service provision systems, we analyzed whether the BLL and the SOC have or have not used the indicators and dimensions included in Table 8.1.

From this analysis, some results and conclusions are now drawn.

Both systems largely exploit ICT to achieve their goals, but the service provisioning models are quite different. BLL connects public and private operators providing services to job seekers and employers. In such a system, a CV or a job offer posted to a public employment office or to an agency is shared among all the operators that are part of the federation.

BLL leverages web technologies through which final users can post CVs and job offers with no need for physical presence in front of operators. Analogously, employers can post a job offer on the web. On the other site, the Catalan system is based on a network of public offices not fully collaborating yet with private agencies working in the recruitment area. ICT provides diverse services online, such as information on job offers, CV, training courses, legal roles, administrative procedures for companies and job seekers. The system communicates the list of unemployed persons to the Spanish Government to trigger unemployment contributions and for statistical data, as well as to share information on job offers and CVs. New services and functions have been included during a long period in the BLL and the SOC following the *E-Government maturity model*. BLL was fully active with new functions from 2003 to the end of 2011, when the service was transferred to the Italian Welfare Ministry. Currently, it supports only some basic services out of the large set of services addressing education and professional information. The SOC website became operative in 2006. Several new functions have been implemented since then. Currently, SOC is rather simple in its offered services but effective, possibly due to its ease-of-use and conciseness.

The proposed typology of e-Government stakeholder roles seems to be appropriate to model the existing relationships among users of both the BLL and the SOC. While BLL is based on a coopetitive approach in order to integrate private job agencies (sharing some data and, at the same time, competing in placements), the SOC operating model only recently included private actors, allowing them to participate in a cooperative way since then. The main stakeholders are companies, citizens, unemployed people, redundancy payment recipients, PA staff (employment

Table 8.1 Our proposed assessment indicators

Dimensions	Sub-dimensions	Indicators
Strategic	Strategy definition and control	Definition of objectives and success level control
	Risk management	Reduced risk factors
	Decision-making quality	Number of decisions and alternatives Time required for decision
Economic and financial	Benefit/cost ratio ROI	Identification and measurement of components Return on investment for a project or system ratio
	Cost system effectiveness	Reductions of the overall and unit costs
	Efficiency	Economies of scale gains Time to process a standard case
Organizational and technological	Structure	Re-designed business process Number of formalized processes Hierarchical levels and staff participation
	Strengthening human capital	Increased efficiency, resource rationalization, greater productivity, etc. Time savings Competent and skilled staff achieving greater output Stakeholders' and users' involvement and co-production
	Integration	Online exchanged documents ICT infrastructure coherence score ICT enabled face-to-face contact points
	Accessibility	Usage by disadvantaged groups SMEs bidding for public tenders online
	The system and ICT infrastructure	Nature of back office changes Services available online Privacy rating for websites Usability score Public agencies with integrated ICT financial and resource planning
Service provision social	Service quality	New access channels and choice Stakeholders involvement Transparency, accountability, etc., for users
	Information usefulness	Users getting information Validity, accuracy, sufficiency, timeliness, reliability, relevancy
	Satisfaction—fulfilment	Time saved for citizens and business Service fulfilment (problem solved) User-satisfaction (citizens, companies, staff) index
	Fairness	Justice and security ratings Fairness of service provision
	Trust and confidence in government	Transparency, accountability, security, privacy, etc.
	Development	Developing learning and skills Employment and jobs

(continued)

Table 8.1 (continued)

Dimensions	Sub-dimensions	Indicators
Political and democratic	Openness	Response time to online queries Policy drafts available online Processes open online (tendering, procurement, etc.)
	Transparency and accountability	Processes fully traceable online Public agencies reporting their budget and expenditure online Services involving a two-way interaction with users
	Participation	Accessibility rating of sites and participation Contributions to online discussion forums Queries submitted online Feedback Co-production of services

services, social security, etc.- at different geographical levels), governments (Regional, National, and European), training companies, institutions, private employment agencies, and portals of other PA institutions.

8.4   Case Study: Services for Social Care of Frail Subjects (Attiv@bili)

For health care managers, the effective care of frail patients is becoming a crucial application of e-Government. Frail patients, according to (Fried et al. 2001) include elderly people and people with disabilities, requiring both health care and social care services provided at home and in residential, assisted locations. Frail people need to live as much as possible in their household, with the support of ICT tools and home automation devices increasing quality of life and safety, coherently with the current topic of smart cities and communities and of social inclusion.

Attiv@bili[1] addresses health care and social care services, supporting patients' everyday life (e.g., accompanying, housekeeping, food, transportation) and services for improved communication and social inclusion. The project focuses on organizational features for process coordination among organizations and on ICT integrated solutions. ICT is a key factor to build a sustainable proposal of integration, in that it can enable correct and effective information exchange among the involved

---

[1]Attiv@bili is a Research Project (Sept 2014–Dec 2015) in the area of Industrial Research, framed in the call "Avviso pubblico per la realizzazione di progetti di ricerca industriale e sviluppo sperimentale nel settore delle Smart Cities and Communities", approved by Regione Lombardia—DGR 2760/13 in the Action "Smart Cities and Communities"—POR FESR 2007–2013.

caregivers, improve business process management, and empower innovative smart living tools.

In social care for frail persons, co-production incorporates strengthened roles for families, neighbors, and communities to provide caring, encouragement and social activities. In other words, in this context the health and well-being of the person in care depend on more elements than a one-to-one relationship between the frail person and the caregiver. From this perspective, Attiv@bili employs ICT advancement such as Ambient Intelligence, and Interactive Social Media that facilitate communication between patients and the family, friends, neighbors and supporting patient's social interaction through social networking tools (e.g., interactive television and social agents).

Figure 8.1 shows the architecture of the Attiv@bili project that connects the frail person with the local health authority, municipality for social care and with the family, friends, neighbors and volunteers by developing web-based platforms. The platform developed to enable co-production, allows the co-producers and the organizer entities to communicate and share information. The environment and patient are monitored using sensors in the environment or wearable sensors carried by the patient. The aim is to detect risks such as failure, absence of the patient from home for a long time (e.g., for elderly with Alzheimer's disease), and environmental and safety risks, such as gas leak, fire, etc. In this way, the volunteered neighbors or family and friends can be informed in case of a problem that can be handled by non-expert persons. If the risk requires an expert intervention, the emergency center and/or the caregiver are notified to intervene accordingly.

In Table 8.2, we compare the two use cases, considering the adoption of elements that facilitate co-production in e-Government services. The issues considered for this comparison are a mix between what we have presented in the previous

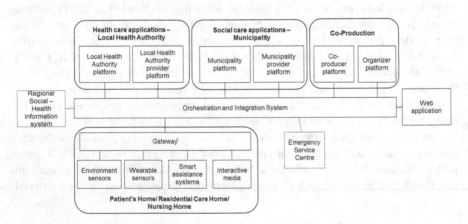

Fig. 8.1 Architecture of the Attiv@bili ICT platform. Modified from Attiv@bili WP2 and WP6 Technical Reports, 2015

Table 8.2 Comparing e-Government use cases considering elements that facilitate co-production

Elements facilitating co-production	SOC	BLL	Attiv@bili
Involving stakeholders and users from the start	No	No	Yes
Rewarding co-producers	No	No	No
Cost-reduction through ICT technology	Yes	Yes	No
Easy-to-use and accessible communication means	Yes	Yes	Yes
Considering diversity	Yes	Yes	Yes
ICT platform can be used easily by non-technical users	Yes	No	No
Built on top of existing platforms	Yes	Yes	No
Platforms for gathering user feedback, report and opinions	Yes	No	No
Providing training for co-producers	No	No	Yes
Organization of co-production activities	No	No	Yes
Privacy and security	Yes	Yes	Yes

section and the elements characterizing co-production, as from the literature presented in Chap. 1.

In what follows, we review those ICT advances that can play a critical role in facilitating co-production in e-Government services, with examples of their adoption in the case studies. The list is not exhaustive, obviously, since other technologies are being delivered, typically regarding the web or ambient assisted living technologies, to mention just a few, which are likely to change the face of many aspects related to services. We consider those, which, in our opinion, are mature enough to make the difference in e-Government and in co-production.

8.5 What Is ICT Offering?

Authors in (Linders and Copeland Wilson 2011) examine whether the *tools of the information age* make citizen co-production in e-Government services more viable and effective. The paper discusses the re-emergence of citizen co-production as a fashionable policy option in spite of persistent budget deficits, of the rise of "government by network", and of the advent of mass "peer-production". Then, it applies this framework to evaluate the impact of ICT tools on citizen co-production. It claims that Internet-based tools enable new forms of citizen co-production, such as *Do-It-Yourself Government* and *Government as a Platform*. The same author, in (Linders 2012) examines the evolution of citizen co-production in the age of social media, web 2.0 interactivity, and ubiquitous connectivity.

The basic innovative ICT tools and paradigms and their use in facilitating co-production are discussed in the following.

8.5.1 Communication and Hardware ICT Infrastructures

In this part, we review the communication and hardware infrastructures advances, and their role in co-production and more specifically, we discuss examples where they can be incorporated in the use cases mentioning their advantages and limitations.

8.5.1.1 Internet of Things (IoT) and Smart Cities

According to (Harmon et al. 2015), Internet of Things (IoT) refers to the networked interconnection of everyday objects, which, equipped with ubiquitous intelligence, form smart environments, e.g., smart cities. IoT is opening many opportunities for a large number of novel applications that can improve the quality of life in many domains, such as transportation and logistics, healthcare, personal and social domains. Authors in (Oliveira and Campolargo 2015) discuss new governance models that allow collaboration of citizens in smart cities for co-production of user-centered smart services that encourage the citizens to be the *driver of change* in face of major city challenges.

Co-production in IoT-Services fosters a vision on how citizens and the public sector can cooperate in deciding how smart the environment should be, selecting what should be monitored, through which smart devices, which IoT-Services are needed and how they should be delivered. IoT-Service provisioning is a knowledge intensive procedure that involves sensing many aspects in the environment. Co-production in this regard can consider the citizens as a source of knowledge gathering. They are either actors, who detect the issues of the infrastructures, improving the services based on citizen's feedbacks or actors who use the sensing data sent by the IoT-Services.

Citizens can be involved in sensing procedures needed for IoT by being equipped with the basic sensors and devices on their smart phones, such as accelerometers, localization sensors and so on. On the other hand, the communities of users can help in maintaining the smart city processes by providing feedbacks on features such as efficiency and other quality parameters. They can contribute through *social platforms* connected to the IoT systems in developing a network of alerts and reports such as event detection and reaction, and reports on privacy violations or crimes, for instance. Furthermore, IoT enables easier access to social programs for citizens e.g., ensuring that organizations can deliver citizen-centered services including care and employment services.

By providing the services that help the co-producer to perform the allocated tasks in a more convenient way, IoT can be considered as one of the ICT advancement in co-production. This technology does not seem particularly relevant for the *employment services* cases. On the other side, IoT provides interconnected communication and enhanced sensing and monitoring as done in the context of *Attiv@bili*. Trusted family members and friends can be authorized to gain remote access to control some elements in the patient's environment. As an example, in case a gas leak is detected in the patients house, the family member can be informed and remotely close the gas flow using the sensing and control functionalities made available by IoT-Services.

However, privacy and security are a concern in order to avoid unpermitted monitoring of sensitive data or patient's information to be accessed by unauthorized entities. Furthermore, IoT-Services for sensing and controlling critical sensors and devices, such as the patient's heart monitor, should be managed with care (e.g., an unauthorized entity accessing the heart monitor might give a heart shock to the patient with severe consequences).

8.5.1.2 Mobility

With portable computers, mobile phones, tablets, smart cards, and wearable computers, the ability to communicate has revolutionized the perspective on information and communication systems. Mobile data communication has become a very important, rapidly evolving and convolving technology as it allows users to transmit data from remote locations to other remote or fixed locations that solves the problem of mobility. Today's mobile phones are equipped with sophisticated sensors, and advanced computing powers, while wearable devices are becoming more intelligent with increased processing capabilities (Pejovic and Musolesi 2015):

Smart mobile devices can supply smart interfaces to access PA systems from various locations and encourage co-production of simple, micro services developed by communities of users. Mobility enables and enhances the involvement of citizens anywhere they are, through access to a smart phone. Moreover, the development of mobile applications has become very easy and low cost while they can be easily accessed and used by non-technical users. This can encourage the PAs to develop the means required by the co-production style of using mobile applications, such as knowledge gathering, communication between citizens and the PAs, crime and accident reporting, and so on.

Security is a concern also in this case, since mobile devices can be moved anywhere by anyone, can be potentially influenced by the environment where they are located, and can be stolen or lost. Therefore, they need to be protected adequately by passwords or other authentication techniques for security and privacy of information accessible on the device. On the other hand, the security measures should not be a burden in use, since one of the advantage points of adopting smart mobile devices is their availability and ease of use.

By using mobile applications, it is possible to develop low-cost, easy to access platforms for co-producer's communication that can be used anywhere in our use cases. By improving the communication of co-producers and PA, the organization of co-production activities can be facilitated. Moreover, the users can be encouraged in getting involved in co-production as the platforms in this way can be more accessible and user friendly. One issues of mobile applications regards *diversity*, as not all the users own or know how to use a smart-phone properly. Therefore, this technology should be used in combination with other technologies (e.g., portable computers or TV) to meet the requirement of diversity for facilitating co-production.

8.5.1.3 Cloud Computing

Authors in (Nazir et al. 2015) introduce cloud computing as a model for enabling ubiquitous, convenient, on-demand network access to a shared pool of configurable computing resources with a leased basis and the ability to scale up and down based on service requirements. Cloud services change the way that computing resources are perceived, purchased and consumed. In fact, they shift the attention from IT resources as tangible goods to *IT resources as a service.*

In this way, the cloud can facilitate the adoption of co-production by enabling simple and easy data sharing among different stakeholders, reducing the IT resources costs, providing a globally available services to anyone (if properly authorized), anywhere, and by eliminating IT complexities from the end user's part.

Co-production can foster on cloud computing where the communities of co-producers, experts, and PAs can attain to the cloud as a source of services that facilitates the collaboration while reducing the costs.

Moreover, the main characteristics of the cloud makes it a great choice for e-Government applications such as SOC, BLL and Attiv@bili. *On demand self-service* enables the organizations to use computing capabilities on demand, which make it easy to add the new platforms needed for co-production. *Broad network access* makes services available globally over the network that can be accessed via standard mechanisms that increases the accessibility of the platform for co-producers. Last but not the least, *rapid elasticity* provides the capability to scale quickly based on the resources needed at any time. This capability is highly enabling since in co-production the need for resources and interactions of the users can change in time (e.g., during an environmental crisis, like a hurricane, there can be a peak in amount of communications from the citizens for reporting the crisis).

Privacy of data shared on the cloud is an important issue. Sharing knowledge and skills in co-production is also something that needs to be protected from undesired disclosure and with the user consent. Solutions are usually based on single-sign-on technology and cryptography, although fast access and ease-of-use still limit the application of cryptography.

8.5.2 The World Wide Web

We review the ICT advances over word wide web and their role and influence on e-Government and co-production. Moreover, with a special focus on services for employment and Attiv@bili, we discuss in which sense they can be adopted, what are the advantages they introduce and what are their shortcomings and limitations for these specific cases.

8.5.2.1 Semantic Web

The Semantic Web is an extension of the web through standards, where information has a well-defined meaning, better enabling computers and people to work in cooperation (Mika and Greaves 2012). It is a source to retrieve information form the web, and access the data through Semantic Web Services. For the Semantic Web to operate, computers must have access to structured collections of information and sets of inference rules that can be used to conduct automated reasoning.

The Semantic Web provides a common framework that allows the data to be shared and reused across applications, enterprise and community boundaries, as needed for co-production and e-Governance.

Moreover, the machine readable descriptions of knowledge enable co-producers play the role of content managers to add meaning to the content, i.e., to describe the structure of knowledge. In this way, a machine can process knowledge itself, instead of the text, using deductive reasoning and inference, thereby obtaining more meaningful results, and helping computers to perform automated information gathering and search. On the other hand, ontologies and other paradigms used for representing the semantics in the web can be fed and populated by different categories of users as co-producers, under the umbrella of well-defined categories of concepts where homonyms and synonyms are solved via thesauri or dictionaries allowing avoiding inconsistencies.

In our use cases, volunteered users as co-producers, can have the task of annotating the data that need to be processed. In this way, the analysis of these data can be automated and PA can save time and costs needed for expert involvements in processing of data. In services for employment, the data regard the CV and job offers posted by job seekers and enterprises. In Attiv@bili, these data are gathered from the environment and the person in care via sensors, and represent the situations that are present in each time. Another use of the semantic web in the context of these two projects is *sentiment analysis* of the user feedbacks, reports and posts in social media, forums and communities to understand the level of user satisfaction of the services and to drive the important feedbacks that can help in improving the services.

8.5.2.2 Web Services

Web services are applications accessible to other applications over the web, which are self-contained, modular business applications with open, internet-oriented, standard interfaces (Zimmermann et al. 2012). Employing the Service Oriented Architecture (SOA), web services are defined as loosely coupled units, which can be combined with other services and accessed and used by provided interfaces without the need to have knowledge about the implementation of services.

Web services have changed the market conditions towards cost-effectiveness and facilitating the reuse and interconnection of the existing IT assets (Lippert and Govindarajulu 2015). Since the same standards are adopted in defining the data descriptions and connection protocols, the need for costly and time-consuming reprogramming of the existing applications can be reduced. Therefore, even in case of frequent changes to the requirements, it is much easier to shift the perspectives of the organizations into co-production.

Co-production can benefit from web services and from the SOA by adopting the standard-based models and architectures that, through their loose coupling characteristics, increase modularity and flexibility in distributed ICT infrastructures needed in these cases. In this way, new platforms, needed for incorporating co-production, can be built on top of the existing (legacy) platforms. Moreover, web services can improve the upgrading process of systems while reducing the integration costs and simplifying business-to-business integration, facilitating co-production between organizations and other entities.

In addition, by adopting web services and the SOA as the basis for services for employment and Attiv@bili, different, heterogeneous systems are enabled to incorporate co-production in a platform-independent environment, and to access the databases of the adhering entities (local PAs, private entities, institutions). In this case, different entities are able to share their data and services with co-producers, while they can conserve their systems and technologies.

8.5.3   Information, Data Management, Innovation

In this part, we discuss the role of data management in e-Government and co-production. Moreover, we discuss how data can turn into knowledge that can be incorporated in e-Government services.

8.5.3.1   Big Data and Knowledge Management Systems

Big data is a concept used to describe data sets that cannot be processed using traditional data processing tools and techniques (Mayer-Schonberger and Cukier 2013). For a data set to be considered as big data, the following characteristics, called *4 Vs*, are considered: *Volume*, the quantity and the size of the data set; *Variety*, the type of the content (e.g., image, voice, video, text, etc.); *Velocity*, the speed at which the data is generated and processed; and *Veracity*, the uncertainty of data.

A big data item has high volume, high velocity, and/or high variety and veracity. Big data introduce many challenges regarding the capturing, analysis, maintenance, search, sharing, storage, transfer and visualization of the data. Succeeding in the analysis of big data greatly improves finding new correlations in the huge amount of data that are available in the web, e.g., in organizational and public administration records, and that can help to spot the trends, finding the patterns to make sense of large amounts of data.

On the other hand, big data need to be transformed into knowledge to be able to incorporate them in different areas and to manage knowledge. *Knowledge management* can be simply defined as the process of getting the most out of knowledge resources (Becerra-Fernandez and Sabherwal 2014). It is the process of capturing, sharing and leveraging knowledge efficiently for the aim of improving performance, innovation, and information sharing, which are important aspects in co-production.

Knowledge sharing that is facilitated using knowledge management strategies can enhance decision-making by supporting co-production in knowledge creation. Knowledge sharing can positively affect services for employment by empowering the job seekers and employers towards self-management and establishment of involvement of users to co-produce the knowledge bases representing various aspects of the job market. This in turn can be used to enhance the services for training according to the needs of the job market to reduce the gap between trained skills of the workers and requirements in the job market.

In Attiv@bili, big data analysis and visualization enhance the non-expert co-producer's ability in understanding the knowledge shared to execute their tasks. As in this project, huge amounts of data are gathered from the environment, the patient in care, and also considering the available knowledge bases that should be shared with the co-producers, big data analysis come as a solution to extract the relevant knowledge from the available data. Moreover, visualization of data can incorporate security, and privacy techniques to protect the sensitive information from being viewed by unauthorized entities involved in co-production.

On the other hand, the use of data-intensive technologies and big data in platforms which enable co-production allow for cost reduction and improve productivity and innovation by making available the required knowledge that needs to be shared with co-producers.

Co-production in our definition also includes knowledge gathering from users as co-producers. The analysis of data gathered from users of the systems can help to detect trends and requirements, such as needs of frail people, or competences of the caregivers. The anlaysis can also help supporting the role of environment, the social interactions and the patients' involvement in social interactions, the quality of the patients' life, their overall health, happiness and wellbeing. In the case of employment services, data analysis and co-production are related in that the trends in the job market, the role of education in finding jobs and so on can be studied. Detecting the gaps between the job market needs and worker's trainings based on historical data helps to improve training and education systems to match the requirements and skills. Moreover, big data analytics results in turning large amounts of data into knowledge that facilitates the identification of requirements, service provisioning, prediction and prevention of potential problems and the generation of reports and feedbacks of users in different aspects, such as level of satisfaction about a service.

8.5.3.2 Crowdsourcing and Open Innovation

Crowdsourcing is a concept defining the common effort of a group of interested people to solve a given problem with the explicit intention to access their diversified knowledge (Thapa et al. 2015). The collaborative aspect of crowdsourcing enhances the quality, range, and outcome of the solutions and leads to new innovative ideas that can be employed by the public and the private sectors. Crowdsourcing can aim to perform simple and routine tasks or to generate innovative solutions for complex problems employing the collaborative efforts of the crowd.

One of the most relevant examples of crowdsourcing for public and private organizations is Open Innovation (Belenzon and Schankerman 2015). With the increased opportunities to work with external partners, firms started to move towards "Open Innovation" leaving behind the previously popular business model of closed innovation that limited the organization in using internal resources for new product development. Open innovation encourages the paradigm "connect & develop" which adopts the external sources of ideas with a higher priority than those generated by the internal resources, or as their complement to create great value. The public sector can benefit from open innovation by leveraging the external knowledge sources to add public value, without the limitations on the capacity for continuous improvements and adaptation that previously was an obstacle. Furthermore, community-led open innovation can involve citizens in collaborative projects as needed in co-production and e-Government paradigms.

Crowdsourcing and Open Innovation facilitate service provision rapidly from a broad network of individuals and institutions. Using the "Wisdom of the Crowd", new ideas can be incorporated in co-production and e-Government with low costs. Public services such as medicine have already adopted crowdsourcing, e.g., in Medicine 2.0/ Health 2.0 that are examples incorporating Crowdsourcing and Open Innovation to improve collaboration and to personalize health care (Boudry 2015).

Co-production comes in an agile form of enhanced user interaction in creating, maintaining, commenting services. One problem could be the fastness of acknowledging the co-production processes from the PA side, while peer-to-peer co-production is facilitated by the presence of tools that enhance sharing of very practical knowledge about procedures, small business processes, or comments about services provided to well defined communities exhibiting common needs and expertise level.

In services for employment and in Attiv@bili, this paradigm allows one to extract and use external resources, knowledge and skills from various entities, to implement new social care and employment services and platforms. As the budget for these e-Government applications is limited, it is of great help to use Crowdsourcing and Open Innovation as low-cost tools that encourage citizens' involvement as co-producers for service provisioning and enhancement of existing services.

8.5.3.3   Social Networks and Gamification

Social networks and media comprises new technologies aimed at providing virtual environments that enable data exchange in a dynamic and distributed way. Authors in (Feeney and Welch 2014) and (Mainka et al. 2014) show that social media are increasingly being used in public administrations and e-Government to foster user interaction. Social networks encourage and enhance participation and knowledge production. Moreover, they can improve collaboration of different entities towards a common goal that is needed in co-production.

Furthermore, by replacing or coupling social media technology with the traditional structural and authority infrastructures, it is possible to encourage social collaboration and communication of the person in care with the caregivers, family, friends, communities, and other frail people. In this way, the co-producers can communicate easily with the person in care through social media platforms and provide encouragement and support that can improve the person's well-being. Similarly, in services for employment, social networks provide the low-cost platforms needed for communication between co-producers and organization entities in PA.

Another powerful technology that can be coupled with social media is gamification. Games can be powerful experiences that leverage the motivation and engagement of the players toward a goal (Robson et al. 2015). In co-production, gamification leverages game design elements and game principles in non-game contexts, where the main goal is to produce a gameful experience in order to improve user engagement and productivity in contexts such as producing innovation and ideas, finishing assigned tasks and data gathering. By targeting human's natural desires such as socializing, learning, sense of achievement and success, competition, and finding closure, gamification aims at encouraging and engaging the players to finish certain tasks. In addition, gamification can be used for knowledge gathering from the patients in a more pleasant and interesting way, getting their attention and encouraging their collaboration for enhancing care services based on their feedbacks. Feedback forms can be designed using gamification by adding narratives and adding meaning to the choices. Furthermore, the training procedures for co-producers in our use cases can be enhanced by adding gamification strategies.

8.6   Conclusions

This chapter has discussed how e-Government can be supported and boasted through ICT for co-production. Two use cases have been presented: services for employment and services for social care for frail people, with a comparison of their co-production elements and the involvement of users and stakeholders. ICT advances in improving and incorporating co-production elements in the use-cases have been analyzed.

Co-production in public services of e-Government offers various ideas that emerge when considering:

- the skills and expertise in ICT required for getting users engaged in co-producing services, both as individuals and in partnership with other stakeholders;
- the interoperability frameworks and platforms required to handle inter-organizational processes and structures to enable co-production;
- the critical ICT components (network, web services, smart mobility components, security tools, knowledge management tools) needed for co-producing public services.

The relevance of user-friendly and modern suites of tools is straightforward. An interesting debate regards understanding whether ICT tools are useful (efficient, effective, productive, and so on) in all the life cycle of services and therefore could benefit of co-production in the various phases, or, if conversely, they are crucial for some phases only (e.g., design).

Another issue regards the maintenance of a co-produced ICT-based system, its complexity and the role of public managers and public stakeholders in the maintenance process.

Finally, the impact of technology on the quality of the developed services seems to be an open issue deserving investigation, as well as the privacy and trust aspects involved in co-production related to the developed services. One issue connected with ICT solutions regards problems of *security and privacy*. Security solutions, such as cryptosystems or cybersecurity measures, should be carefully designed also involving end users, through a—possibly easy—explanation of the burdens that protection techniques (e.g., cryptography) imply.

A challenge could be *co-production of security services*, by adopting the consumers' needs on the one side and the providers/PAs norms and laws on the other.

In general, we point out that ICT alone is not sufficient to provide better services nor to involve users in working in co-production. An early and thorough user involvement, together with a political and organizational support, are needed if true co-production styles are to be promoted.

References

J. Alford. *Engaging public sector clients. From Service Delivery to Co-production* (s.l., Palgrave Macmillan, Houndmills, Hamps and New York, NY, 2009)

I. Becerra-Fernandez, R. Sabherwal, *Knowledge Management Systems and Processes* (Routledge, s.l., 2014)

S. Belenzon, M. Schankerman, Motivation and sorting of human capital in open innovation. Strateg. Manag. J. **32**(6), 795–820 (2015)

L. Bettencourt, A. Ostrom, S. Brown, R. Roundtree, 22 Client Co-production in knowledge-intensive business services. Oper. Manage. Strateg. Approach (2005)

C. Boudry, Web 2.0 applications in medicine: trends and topics in the literature. Med. 2.0, JMIR Publ. **4**(1) (2015)

S.E. Colesca, Understanding trust in e-Government. Eng. Econ. **63**(4) (2015)

M.K. Feeney, E.W. Welch, *Technology-Task Coupling Exploring Social Media Use and Managerial Perceptions of e-Government* (The American Review of Public Administration, s.l., 2014)

L.P. Fried et al., Frailty in older adults: evidence for a phenotype. J. Gerontol. Ser. A Biol. Sci. Med. Sci. **56**(3) (2001)

M.G. Fugini, F. Cirilli, P. Locatelli, Integrated care solutions. ERCIM News (102) (2015)

M.G. Fugini, P. Maggiolini, R. Salvador Vallés, *e-Government and Employment Services: A Case Study in Effectiveness* (s.l., SpringerBriefs in Applied Sciences and Technology, PoliMI SpringerBriefs, 2014)

R.R. Harmon, E.G. Castro-Leon, S. Bhide, *Smart cities and the Internet of Things* (s.l., Portland International Conference on Management of Engineering and Technology (PICMET), IEEE, 2015)

J.T.H. Jaafar, N. Hamza, B.E.M. Hassan, H.A. Hefny, A proposed security model for e-Government based on primary key infrastructure and fingerprints. Egypt. Comput. Sci. J. **38**(2) (2014)

K.C. Laudon, J.P. Laudon, *Essentials of Management Information Systems*. Upper Saddle River: Pearson (2011)

D. Linders, From e-government to we-government: defining a typology for citizen co-production in the age of social media. Gov. Inf. Q. **29**(4), 446–454 (2012)

D. Linders, S. Copeland Wilson, *What is open government? One year after the directive*. s.l., 12th Annual International Digital Government Innovation in Challenging Times (ACM, 2011), pp. 262–271

S.K. Lippert, C. Govindarajulu, Technological, organizational, and environmental antecedents to web services adoption. Commun. IIMA **6**(1) (2015)

A. Mainka, S. Hartmann, W.G. Stock, I. Peters, *Government and Social Media: A Case Study of 31 Informational World Cities*. s.l., 47th Hawaii International Conference on System Sciences (HICSS) (IEEE, 2014), pp. 1715–1724

V. Mayer-Schonberger, K. Cukier, *Big Data: A Revolution that will Transform How we Live, Work, and Think* (Houghton Mifflin Harcourt, s.l., 2013)

A. Meijer, e-Governance innovation: barriers and strategies. Gov. Inf. Q. **32**(2), 198–206 (2015)

P. Mika, M. Greaves, Editorial: semantic web & web 2.0. Web Semant. Sci. Serv. Agents World Wide Web **6**(1) (2012)

M. Nazir, P. Tiwari, S.D. Tiwari, R.G. Mishra, *Cloud Computing: An Overview*. In: Cloud Computing: Reviews, Surveys, Tools, Techniques and Applications (s.l.: HCTL Open, 2015)

A. Oliveira, M. Campolargo, *From Smart Cities to Human Smart Cities*. s.l., 48th Hawaii International Conference on System Sciences (HICSS) (IEEE, 2015)

V. Pejovic, M. Musolesi, Anticipatory mobile computing: a survey of the state of the art and research challenges. ACM Comput. Surv. **47**(3) (2015)

K. Robson et al., *Is It All a Game? Undereestanding the Principles of Gamification* (s.l., Business Horizons, 2015)

B.E. Thapa, B. Niehaves, C. Seidel, R. Plattfaut, Citizen involvement in public sector innovation: government and citizen perspectives. Inf. Polity **20**(1), 3–17 (2015)

O. Zimmermann, M. Tomlinson, S. Peuser, *Perspective on Web Services: Applying SOAP, WSDL, and UDDI to Real-World Projects* (Springer Science & Business Media, s.l., 2012)

Printed in the United States
By Bookmasters

Printed in the United States
By Bookmasters

Printed in the United States
By Bookmasters